South West Mountainbiking

Quantocks • Exmoor • Dartmoor

Vertebrate Graphics

Design and production by Vertebrate Graphics Ltd, Sheffield
www.v-graphics.co.uk

South West
MountainBiking
Quantocks · Exmoor · Dartmoor

Written by
Nick Cotton

South West MountainBiking

Quantocks · Exmoor · Dartmoor

Copyright © 2005 Vertebrate Graphics Ltd/Nick Cotton

Published by **Vertebrate Graphics Ltd**

ISBN 0-9548131-2-X

Cover photo: **Andy Heading**

All other Photography by **Andy Heading**
and **Nick Cotton**

Vertebrate Graphics

Design and production by Nathan Ryder – Vertebrate Graphics Ltd.
Map illustrations by Vertebrate Graphics Ltd.

www.**v-graphics**.co.uk

PLEASE GIVE WAY TO HORSES AND PEDESTRIANS.

Contents

ROUTE GRADES ▲ = MEDIUM ▲ = HARD ▲ = EXTREME (SEE PAGE XII)

KEY TO THE MAP SYMBOLS

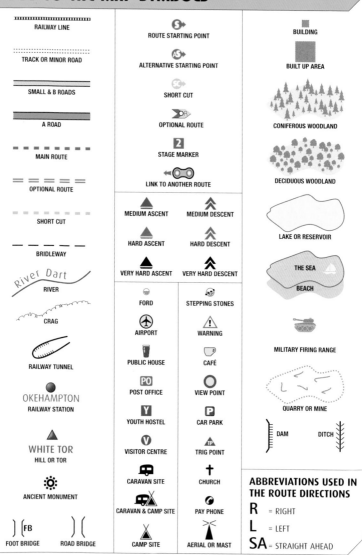

RAILWAY LINE

TRACK OR MINOR ROAD

SMALL & B ROADS

A ROAD

MAIN ROUTE

OPTIONAL ROUTE

SHORT CUT

BRIDLEWAY

River Dart
RIVER

CRAG

RAILWAY TUNNEL

OKEHAMPTON
RAILWAY STATION

WHITE TOR
HILL OR TOR

ANCIENT MONUMENT

) (FB
FOOT BRIDGE   ) (**ROAD BRIDGE**

S→ ROUTE STARTING POINT

AS→ ALTERNATIVE STARTING POINT

CC SHORT CUT

OR OPTIONAL ROUTE

2 STAGE MARKER

LINK TO ANOTHER ROUTE

MEDIUM ASCENT | **MEDIUM DESCENT**

HARD ASCENT | **HARD DESCENT**

VERY HARD ASCENT | **VERY HARD DESCENT**

FORD | **STEPPING STONES**

AIRPORT | **WARNING**

PUBLIC HOUSE | **CAFÉ**

PO POST OFFICE | **VIEW POINT**

Y YOUTH HOSTEL | **P CAR PARK**

V VISITOR CENTRE | **TRIG POINT**

CARAVAN SITE | **† CHURCH**

CARAVAN & CAMP SITE | **PAY PHONE**

CAMP SITE | **AERIAL OR MAST**

BUILDING

BUILT UP AREA

CONIFEROUS WOODLAND

DECIDUOUS WOODLAND

LAKE OR RESERVOIR

THE SEA

BEACH

MILITARY FIRING RANGE

QUARRY OR MINE

DAM | **DITCH**

ABBREVIATIONS USED IN THE ROUTE DIRECTIONS

R = RIGHT

L = LEFT

SA = STRAIGHT AHEAD

Introduction

Dartmoor, Exmoor and the Quantocks offer some of the finest mountain biking in England, comparable in quality and variety with anything you'll find in the National Parks of the North.

Dartmoor's scenery is unlike anything else in the country, with strange shaped grey granite tors rising up out of the landscape; streams cutting deep through dingly dell valleys where you expect pixies to be hiding behind every rock and a bleak, grassy moorland plateau as remote and unforgiving as parts of the Pennines - all riddled with tracks and trails to test every ability.

By contrast Exmoor is smaller and more intimate with a denser network of byways and bridleways criss-crossing the moor. The variety is even greater as Exmoor offers rides high up above the coast as well as tracks over high heather moorland, climbs and descents to make your heart sing and a plethora of pretty villages with pubs and tea shops to satisfy the hungriest appetite. A speciality of the region is the rollercoaster stone stream beds - punctuated with serial drop-offs, they get better each time you ride them.

The Quantock Hills are quite extraordinary - less than 10 miles long and 4 miles wide, they pack in well over a hundred miles of trails on well-drained tracks through gorse, heather and woodland from the broad and easy ridge trail to excellent testing twisty singletrack. Very much a place to explore over and over, perfecting your own circuits as you work through the myriad options.

Just for good measure we have also thrown in a route on the Mendips, the great whaleback of limestone to the south of Bristol.

So, take your pick, explore, enjoy, tell your friends. We aim to please so if you find anything wrong with this guide why not contact us at: **www.v-graphics.co.uk**

Nick Cotton

Acknowledgments

The author would like to thank the following people for support and assistance: Paul Hawkins at Exmoor National Park, Anna Baness at Dartmoor National Park, Ian and Anne Piper at Exmoor House, Porlock.

Vertebrate Graphics would like to thank the following people for their assistance in the production of this guide: Nick Cotton, Andy Heading, Ian and Sandra Dring, Paul Sobczyk, Sheena Law, Pete Alekna, Rhian Manley, Kay Faulkner, Jonathan Hurrell.

Rights of Way

To the best of our knowledge, all of the routes in this guide are totally legal, in other words, mountain bikers have what is termed 'Right of Way'. The following information is provided to help ensure that your ride is legal should you need to adapt your route (shorten or extend your ride) or if you're planning a route of your own from your OS map.

All outdoor folk, including mountain bikers, have to stick to rights of way. Unlike Sweden or Germany, for example, we're not allowed just to wander around the great outdoors willy-nilly, just as we please.

There are a lot of good reasons for sticking to rights of way – here are just a few:

1. We've not always had the right of access to the countryside that we enjoy today. Some pioneering folk have had to work very hard to gain this access from the landowners and it would be a very bad thing to risk jeopardising this hard-won freedom through careless or ill-informed actions.
2. Technically speaking, you're committing trespass if you ride on a footpath – no matter how wide – and you could be prosecuted by a landowner for any damage caused. Also, most sensible people would rather avoid the embarrassment involved in this kind of encounter or confrontation.
3. Riding on footpaths upsets walkers. Again, not worth the aggro – and they've every right to enjoy their day.
4. Sticking to rights of way helps preserve fragile moorland habitats.
5. Riding through overgrown greenery plays havoc with your cassette and jockey wheels.

Rights of Way Include:

Bridleways

Trails for horses, dudes! Mountain bikers have the right to share bridleways with walkers and horses – but take care, horses spook easily.

Byways Open to All Traffic

Otherwise known as BOATs, these allow all traffic to pass, including vehicles – although, surprisingly, I've yet to see a boat on a BOAT. This means that you may well be sharing the trail with motorcyclists and 4WD enthusiasts – often to be seen enjoying the peace, quiet and fresh air of the countryside.

Forest Tracks and Paths

Officially, you need permission to ride through Forestry Commission land. Often however (as is the case with areas of Croydon Hill, south of Dunster) this permission has already been granted, and the Forestry Commission generally regards cycling favourably. A note of caution – beware of forestry operations, because a fully loaded logging truck could easily dent your bike!

Green Lanes

A non-legal term for an unsurfaced country road. There is some debate at the moment as to who's allowed to use them, but mountain bikers have nothing to worry about at present.

White Roads

Most roads on OS maps have colours that indicate their status, white roads have no colour and so have no recorded right of way status. When looking at the map, these often appear to be farm tracks or private roads when, in fact, they are public highways. Of the estimated 7000km of 'lost' white roads around the UK, many are great, totally legal trails. Unfortunately, you need to check with the definitive map at your local highway authority to be absolutely sure. If in doubt stick to a bridleway marked on your OS map. **NB.** If you're not already familiar with the symbols on your OS map denoting bridleways, footpaths and so on, check out the *Public Rights of Way* in the *Customer Information* section on your map.

Signs

Not all footpaths and bridleways are signed. To make matters more confusing, rights of way can change in status (in other words, some bridleways get 'downgraded' to footpaths and some footpaths get 'upgraded' to bridleways) without the signs being changed. What this means is that there is not necessarily any clear indication 'on the ground' as to whether that wide trail that you want to follow is an illegal footpath or a legal bridleway. That's why it's a good idea to carry an OS map with you on every ride.

Some paths have coloured way-marking arrows, these mean:

Yellow: Footpaths (you're not allowed to ride on footpaths, remember)
Blue: Bridleways
Red: Byways that can be used by everyone

Some forestry areas, such as Croydon Hill, south of Dunster, also have way-marked cycle routes. These colouring systems usually indicate the difficulty of the route – look out for explanatory notices at the roadhead.

Rules of the Off Road

Only hooligans enjoy the stress of conflict. The mountain biking community deserves a big pat on the back for keeping it chill on the hill – let's help keep it that way:

1. Always Ride Legal (see note on rights of way)
2. Ride with consideration for others
3. Give way to horses and pedestrians – avoid natural habitats, animals and crops
4. Close all gates
5. Take your litter home
6. Help keep water sources clean – don't take toilet stops near streams
7. Avoid the risk of fire
8. Keep the noise down
9. Be self sufficient for you and your bike
10. Enjoy the countryside and respect its life and work

Safety

This book is aimed at the fit and technically accomplished mountain biker. Almost all of the routes described are challenging and may include very tough climbs and steep (some potentially dangerous) descents. A complete circuit of most of these routes without a 'foot-down', especially on-sight, will deserve a pat on the back – or even a pint!

Warning

Some of these routes venture into remote mooland terrain. If you are planning to tackle any of these (Oareford & Larkbarrow is a good example) you'll need a bit of what's best described as moorland 'savvy'– particularly on shorter, winter days.

Set out properly equipped and properly clothed, carry plenty of water and ensure that you're properly hydrated. Take your spares, a pump and some food. Even if it's warm in the valley, you'll welcome the extra comfort of a windproof if you're taking a snack stop higher up – and this could help avert the dangers of hypothermia in the event of an accident. Pack a good light-source if there's a risk of finishing in the dark.

The ability to read a map and navigate in poor visibility should also be treated as essential. Riding in a group is safer and usually more fun – make sure that you don't leave the slower members of your party too far behind.

Always allow more time than you think is necessary. Bear in mind that a day out with a big group (say five or more in the party) will incur time penalties, as you'll almost inevitably be dealing with 'mechanicals'.

If you are planning to ride alone, take careful stock of the potential seriousness of an accident – you could be without assistance for a considerable length of time. Always tell someone where you are going and when you plan to get back. If you have a mobile phone then take it with you – but be aware that reception can be patchy.

As the area is justifiably popular with other users (and to minimise demands on the National Health Service) we strongly recommend an aptitude versus attitude approach – in other words, please ride within your ability.

On hot, sunny days, make sure that you slap on that Factor 30+ and always wear your helmet.

Mountain Rescue
In the event of an accident requiring mountain rescue assistance:
Dial 999 and ask for **POLICE – MOUNTAIN RESCUE**

How to Use This Book

This book should provide you with all of the information that you need for an enjoyable, trouble free and successful ride. The following tips should also be of help:

1. We strongly recommend that you invest in these three maps: *Ordnance Survey Explorer® OL9 1:25,000 Exmoor, Ordnance Survey Explorer® OL28 (1:25,000) Dartmoor* and *Ordnance Survey Explorer® 140 (1:25,000) Quantock Hills & Bridgwater*. These are essential even if you are familiar with the area – you may need to cut the ride short or take an alternative route.

2. Choose your route. Consider the time you have available and the abilities/level of experience of all members your party – then read the safety section of this guide.

3. We recommend that you study the route description carefully before setting off. Cross-reference this to your OS map so that you've got a good sense of general orientation in case you need an escape route. Make sure that you are familiar with the symbols used on the maps.

4. Get out there and get dirty.

Grading of Routes

You'll notice that we have graded the routes (and certain key climbs/descents within them) on the basis of the Blue, Red and Black system that appears to be increasingly accepted at mountain bike centres around the UK.

This is roughly similar to the system used in skiing where ▲ = **Medium**, ▲ = **Hard** and ▲ = **Extreme**.

The routes are graded for average summer conditions. In a drought they might feel easier, in the depths of winter after three weeks of freeze/thaw action they might feel a little bit trickier. Consideration has been given to such issues as technical severity, length and remoteness. The grades are subjective, the kind of time you have on a given route, or even a specific downhill or climb, will be dictated by your personal levels of fitness, skill and bottle. We hope that we've achieved a balance in our grading that will meet with the approval of the average, non-specialist rider. At least there should be some value in this for pub debates.

Note: Maps, Descriptions, Distances
While every effort has been made to maintain accuracy within the maps and descriptions in this guide, we have had to process a vast amount of information and we are unable to guarantee that every single detail is correct.

Please exercise caution if a direction appears at odds with the route on the map. If in doubt, a comparison between the route, the description and a quick cross-reference to your OS map (along with a bit of common sense) should help ensure that you're on the right track. Note that distances have been measured off the map – these may not tally with your bike computer as map distances rarely coincide 100% with distances on the ground (and you may have to carry your bike at times).

Please treat stated distances as a guideline only.

Bike Set Up

Tyres
The many rocky descents cry out for tyres of a width of 2"+ with square edge knobbles, run at a sensible pressure to avoid snake-bites. You'll be especially grateful for the extra cushioning if you're riding a hard tail.

Frame and Forks
A full suspension frame is not essential, but it will be found to be a great ally on technical ground and will certainly ease the impact of a long day in the saddle.

Brakes
Disc brakes, in addition to their superb stopping power, offer great reliability in muddy conditions and we're treating them as pretty well essential – especially in the winter. Pads may wear out alarmingly quickly in the gritty conditions so choose a hard-wearing compound or bring spares.

Essential Kit

Maps
Ordnance Survey Explorer® OL9 (1:25,000) Exmoor
Ordnance Survey Explorer® OL28 (1:25,000) Dartmoor
Ordnance Survey Explorer® 112 (1:25,000) Launceston & Holsworthy
Ordnance Survey Explorer® 140 (1:25,000) Quantock Hills & Bridgwater

Hydration Pack
Way better then lugging around water bottles. We've been using *Platypus* hydration packs to avoid getting thirsty.

Clothing
The tried and tested layering system utilising 'technical' fabrics (**not cotton**) in a base layer/fleece/wind- or waterproof shell combination works great, especially in winter. As mountain biking is a very active sport, it's worth setting off just a little on the cool side- this should keep you comfortable on the first section, which is usually uphill. Don't, however, make the mistake of leaving those essential warm layers behind. You'll need them on the descents and during snack breaks. There are a few good companies, for example *Endura* and *Gore*, that manufacture quality cycle clothing that can be relied upon in British conditions.

Gloves
Essential – especially in the event of a spill. Make sure that you've got the gloves to fit the season (winter gloves are uncomfortably sweaty in the summer, summer gloves mean numb fingers and a lack of braking response in the winter).

Other Essentials
Don't leave home without a good pump that you're familiar with, spare inner tubes, puncture repair kit and multi-tool. You will need some trail food too.

Thanks to:

Night Riding

Night riding opens up a whole new world of mountain biking enjoyment. Now it is possible to enjoy a mid-week ride of up to two hours (more if you're carrying extra battery juice) in your favourite off-road playground. Night riding is brilliant fun, but it's a completely different ball game out there on a winter's night and (hardly surprisingly) there are a few risks to be aware of. To help stay out of trouble, here are a few tips:

Lights and Batteries

Invest in the best lighting system that you can afford (we've been using the very excellent *Lumicycle* lights over the winter). A helmet mount is superior to a bar mounting on technical ground. Ensure that your battery is fully charged up before you ride. Carry a secondary light source such as a head torch for emergencies. Ensure that you pack a rear light for road sections and keep it clean of mud.

Route Planning and Safety

Choose your ride on the basis of the manufacturer's minimum battery life and allow extra time – you will be slower in the dark. Stay on ground that you are familiar with at first (night-time navigation in unfamiliar territory demands military expertise) and not too far from major roads. Always ride with a friend. Make sure that someone knows where you're going and when to expect you back.

Ride within your limits – trees loom up very quickly in the dark!

PHOTO COURTESY OF LUMICYCLE

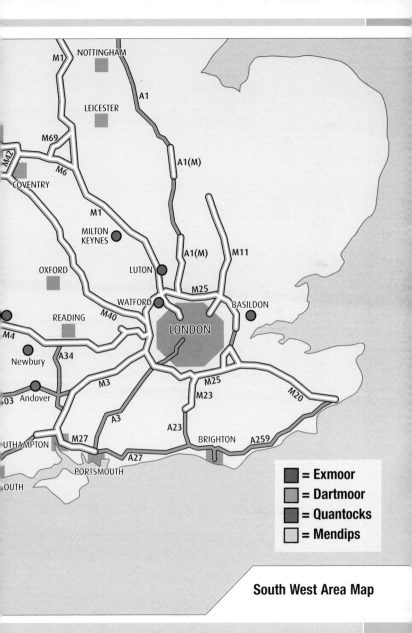

= Exmoor
= Dartmoor
= Quantocks
= Mendips

South West Area Map

Dartmoor

Dartmoor has a fascinating mixture of moorland, forest, dramatic granite tors, Dingly Dell pixieland and old mysterious stones. The mountain biking varies from tangles with tussocks on the high moorland to superb stone-based tracks and everything in between. Despite being much larger than Exmoor, Dartmoor has fewer mountain biking options as there are vast swathes of grassy plateau in the centre where there are no tracks, and other places where a bridleway marked on the map may not correspond to anything on the ground.

Dartmoor
sponsored by  MARIN®

www.marin.co.uk

Do not despair! There are enough tracks around the edges of the moor, and also around the **Princetown/Postbridge** area in the centre, to offer a great selection of rides to test the fittest.

In the north and west the rides explore the edges of the moor from **Okehampton**, **Lydford** and **Peter Tavy**, all of which could be linked up for a mega day out. The one exception to the fringes of the moor rule is the military road loop which climbs right into the heart of the moor to 560m. Although this is also used by the occasional vehicle it has a very different feel to it from a normal mountain bike ride.

In the centre, the bleak grey prison town of **Princetown** is a hub for two rides: down to **Burrator Reservoir** and across open moorland past the atmospheric ruins at **Swincombe** to **Hexworthy**. A little further east, one ride from **Postbridge** explores **Bellever Forest** and crosses rivers via some potentially side-splitting stepping stone crossings. A second ride from **Postbridge** goes past the ruins of the medieval village of **Challacombe** across hillsides laden with ferns and heather. This could easily be linked to the two rides based around **Manaton** and **North Bovey** for another big day out. The **Grimspound** ride is an old favourite, taking in the incredible shapes of **Hound Tor** and more **Dingly Dell** streams and boulders.

The final ride is in the southeast: the ride from **South Brent** taking in **Avon Dam Reservoir** has a series of fast grassy descents that will bring a grin to anyone's face.

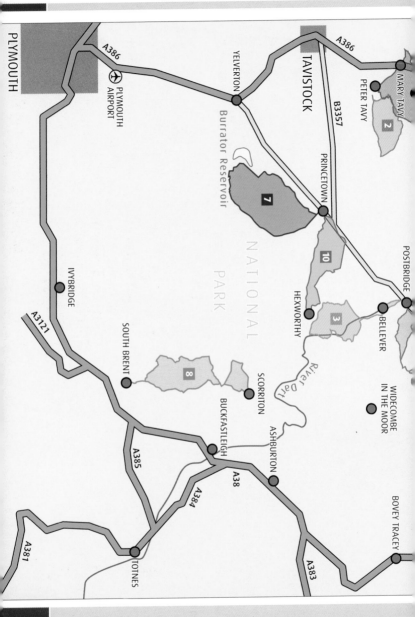

The Dartmoor Area & Routes

1 Granite Way
  & Meldon Reservoir

2 Peter Tavy
  & Merrivale Range

3 Bellever &
  the Stepping Stones

4 Postbridge & Challacombe

5 Grimspound & Hound Tor

6 North Bovey & Foxworthy

7 Princetown to Burrator

8 Avon Dam & Scorriton

9 Lydford & Mary Tavy

10 Princetown & Hexworthy

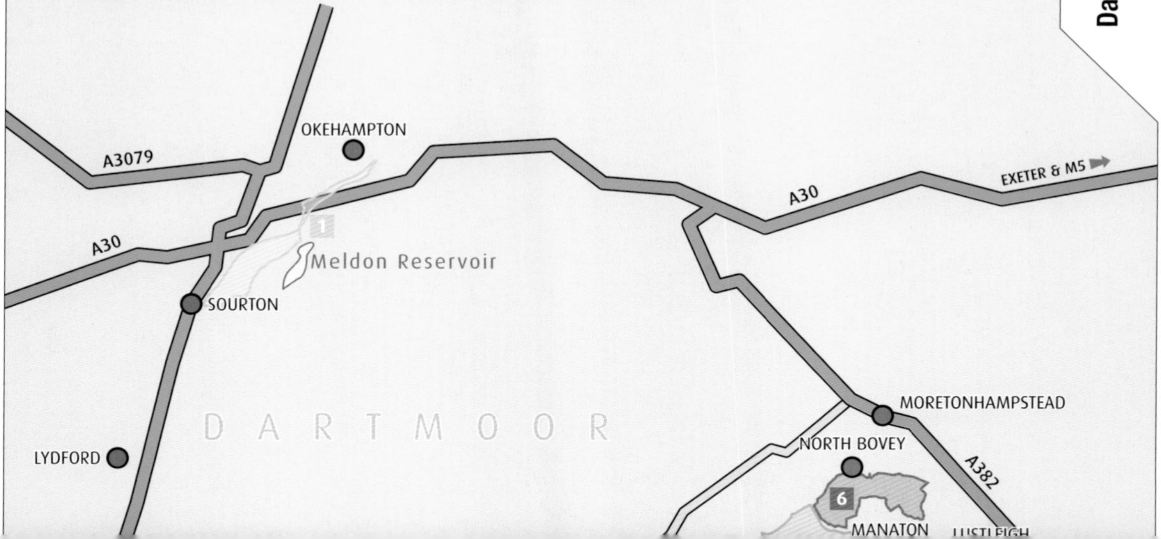

LYDFORD

A30

A3079

SOURTON

Meldon Reservoir

OKEHAMPTON

DARTMOOR

A30

MANATON

NORTH BOVEY

MORETONHAMPSTEAD

A382

LUSTLEIGH

EXETER & M5

Dartmoor Area Map

The Granite Way
& Meldon Reservoir – Dartmoor

Introduction

An easy introduction to the delights of **Dartmoor**, starting off with a converted railway path that is definitely a family ride, the easiest traffic-free section in the whole book, with great views out over **Devon**. After leaving the railway trail, the going gets tougher and there is a testing little descent by the reservoir. Dodging the golf balls on the golf course at the end of the ride adds a little spice to the route.

The Ride

There can be few easier warm-ups than the railway path known as the *Granite Way* that runs for 8km southwest from **Okehampton**. As soon as you leave it the gradient steepens and the surface turns to grass and ferns with the atmospheric *Sourton Tors* ahead. Stone walls, grass tracks and clumps of beech trees define the route towards *Meldon Reservoir*, beyond which the pulse quickens for a steep then easier woodland descent beneath the viaduct and on down to cross the *A30*. Rough pasture leads to the immaculate greens of the golf course followed by tracks and lanes leading back to the café at the start.

Making a day of it

By following the *Granite Way* to its southwestern end, and using a short section of the A386 to regain the railway path (at GR 523872), you arrive in **Lydford**, close to the start of the *Lydford & Mary Tavy* ride at GR 502832. This in turn could link to the *Peter Tavy & Merrivale Range* ride.

THE GRANITE WAY & MELDON RESERVOIR	GRADE: ▲
DISTANCE: 16KM	**TOTAL ASCENT:** 180M
START/FINISH: OKEHAMPTON	**GRID REFERENCE:** 593 944
PARKING: OKEHAMPTON YOUTH HOSTEL	**CAFÉ:** OKEHAMPTON YHA Tel: 01837 53 916
PUBLIC HOUSE: HIGHWAYMAN INN, SOURTON Tel: 01837 861 243	

PHOTO: ANDY HEADING

PHOTO: ANDY HEADING

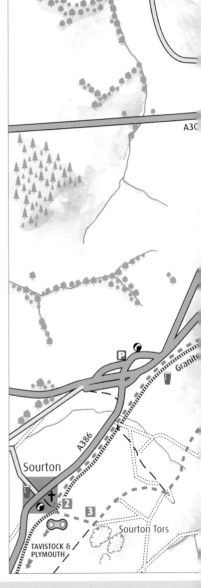

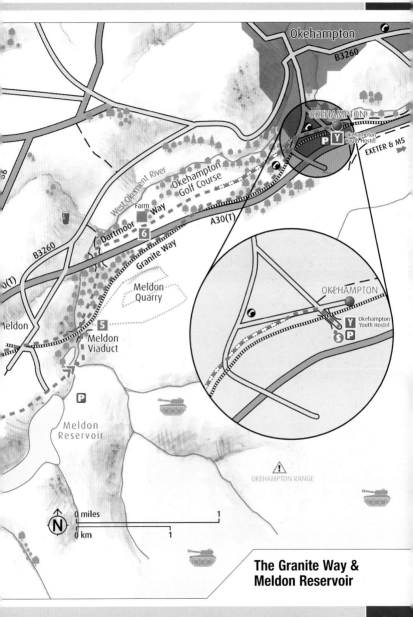

The Granite Way &
Meldon Reservoir

Directions – The Granite Way
& Meldon Reservoir

1   Exit the *YHA* car park, turn **R** under the bridge, then take the first road **L** and shortly turn **L** again onto a zig-zag track leading up to the *Granite Way*, running parallel with the railway line. Pass through the subway, go past old waggons and the quarry, past *Meldon Visitor Centre* and over the viaduct.

2   After 7.5km on this easy trail, at *Sourton Church* (on your right), by a green painted millennium signpost, turn **R** off the railway path then immediately turn sharp **L** uphill to cross the bridge over the railway path. Pass through a gate and follow the stone and grass track towards the distinctive rocks of *Sourton Tors* ahead. At the X-roads of tracks at the top, just beneath the rocks, turn **L** on the less steep of the grassy tracks passing between ferns.

3   Go **SA** at several X-roads of grassy tracks, aiming for the clump of beech trees. The path veers slightly **R** to join a track running alongside the wall (keep the wall to your right) leading to a wooden gate in among the trees with a *West Devon Way* waymark. Go through a second gate at the end of a wide grassy track between stone walls, continue in the same direction, then at a 3-way wooden post bear **R** across the field signposted *Meldon Reservoir* to pass outside the corner of the stone wall. Follow the obvious track with the wall to your left for a short tricky section between rocks.

4   The track becomes wide and grassy with superb views. Descend to cross the road and go **SA** through a gate signposted *Meldon Viaduct*. Very steep descent. Ignore a bridlegate to the right set between two high stone buttresses, then shortly turn **R** over a narrow wooden bridge. Continue **SA** then bear **L** on a wide grassy track to a wooden gate.

5 Emerge at the tarmac directly beneath the viaduct. Turn **L**, then after 100m bear **R** onto a bridlepath. Lovely descent on woodland singletrack. At the road turn **R**, cross the bridge, then take the first wide stone track (driveway) on the **R** to the farm.

6 At the farm fork **R** then climb **R** to go through a gate and follow the path alongside the fence on your left. After a short rough pasture section, go through a gate onto the golf course, following the obvious track **SA** (watch out for golf balls!). The grass track soon turns to gravel then tarmac. After 800m, at the T-junction with a more major road, turn **R** uphill then first **L** (just before road signs) onto a road opposite *Westhill House* to rejoin the outward route and return to the car park at the start.

KAY FAULKNER AND RHIAN MANLEY ENJOY AN EASY CLIMB   PHOTO: ANDY HEADING

EAST FROM PETER TAVY ONTO THE MERRIVALE RANGE   GRADE:

DISTANCE: 13KM	**TOTAL ASCENT:** 330M
START/FINISH: PETER TAVY	**GRID REFERENCE:** 522778
PARKING: CAR PARK EAST OF PETER TAVY CHURCH (GR 522778)	
CAFÉ: BRING SANDWICHES	**PUBLIC HOUSE:** PETER TAVY INN Tel: 01822 810 348

ENJOYABLE 'DARTMOOR STYLE' ROAD WORK **PHOTO:** *ANDY HEADING*

East from Peter Tavy onto the Merrivale Range – Dartmoor

Introduction

For such a short ride this offers almost a full **Dartmoor** spectrum: dingly dell farmland, remote moorland, a military firing range, a standing stone that looks as though it belongs on **Easter Island**, a cracking descent and a good pub at the bottom of the hill. Only problem: see warning above – you may need to choose the right day to ride it.

The ride

The start point is a somewhat improbable little quarry up the hill from *Peter Tavy*. As you turn off the superb stone-based track, you probably think *'Why am I leaving this ideal track?'* Answer: *it is the return route.* So, drop down along field edges and past gnarled old trees with a thousand stories to tell, down past *Broadmoor Farm* to **Cudlipptown** and a gently climbing lane between amazing stone walls. No red flag flying? OK, proceed with caution, and don't start kicking any stray tin cans - mountain biking is easier with both legs intact. The ride gives you a real taste of how bleak and featureless the central plateau of *Dartmoor* can be - a place to be treated with great respect in poor visibility. Boy Scout's motto - always carry a compass. Turning southwest, the path flickers on and off as you pass by the huge standing stone until it becomes much clearer beneath *White Tor* and the fun really begins. Whoooosh!

Making a day of it

This track easily links to the *Lydford & Mary Tavy* ride (and via the *Granite Way* right back to **Okehampton**). Best to start with the *Lydford* ride, leave it shortly after *Hill Bridge* at GR 532801 and turn left towards the heart of the moor to do this loop, then rejoin the *Lydford* ride at **Cudlipptown** (GR 520790). Another option is to use the rough cross-moor bridleway from *Peter Tavy* via *Higher Godsworthy* (GR 530772) to **Merrivale** to link to the *Princetown* rides.

Horndon

Wapsworth

← MARY TAVY

River Tavy

Cudlipptown Down

Cudlipptown

Farm

Smeardon Down

2 Farm

Stephen's
Grave

P
S

Peter
Tavy

Lower Godsworthy

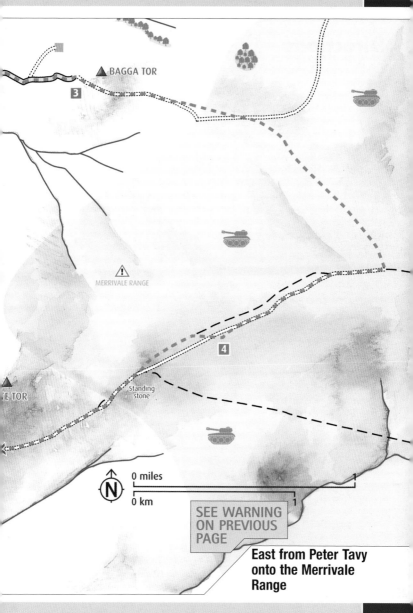

BAGGA TOR

3

⚠ MERRIVALE RANGE

4

E TOR

Standing stone

Ⓝ

0 miles   1

0 km   1

SEE WARNING
ON PREVIOUS
PAGE

**East from Peter Tavy
onto the Merrivale
Range**

**Bellever Forest &
the stepping stones**

Directions – Bellever Forest & the stepping stones

1 Exit the car park and turn **R** towards *Tavistock*. Take the first road **L** signposted *Youth Hostel*, turn **R** into the forest, then fork **L** onto a broad forest road beyond the gate signposted *Public Footpath*.

2 Climb steadily, **ignore** a right turn near the start then after 400m take the **left-hand** track at a fork near a yellow-banded wooden post. Pass through a clearing, then on the descent turn first **L** at a X-roads of tracks signposted *Bridlepath* to continue downhill.

3 Descend through a gate onto a steep rocky track with drainage channels across the path. Go through a second gate and the grassy track turns to tarmac. **Ignore** the first forest road to the right opposite the *Youth Hostel* (this is a private road to *Laughter Hole Farm*). Take the next forest road to the **R** by the *Bellever Forest* signboard signposted *Bridlepath to Laughter Hole Farm*. After 400m go through a bridlegate and bear **L** onto a wide forest road following signs for *Laughter Hole Farm*.

4 Go through a field gate set in a stone wall. After 400m go past a large stone barn, through another gate and bear **R** signposted *Bridlepath, County Road, Huccaby Cottage*. (The track to the left is the return route). Climb to a bridlegate in the stone wall and stay on the main **right-hand** track signposted *Dunnabridge Pound*. Fine open views. Go through a bridlegate and at the road bear **L**.

5 **Easy to miss:** about 70m after crossing the cattlegrid, bear **R** onto a narrow, track by a bridleway post. This is at times tricky with stones (or boulders) on the descent then alongside the river. Cross the river via amazing *'stepping boulders'* (the first of several such crossings). Follow the grassy track (at times faint) parallel with the woodland on the right. More boulder fields.

6 Second stepping stones crossing. Go through a gate and bear **L** onto the road. At the T-junction bear **R** signposted *Holne* (or turn **L** downhill for the *Forest Inn in Hexworthy*). Cross the bridge and climb steeply. As the gradient eases, turn **L** on a broad stone track between rows of stones (there is a blue arrow on a wooden post).

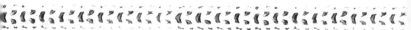

7 The stone track turns to tarmac. About 100m **before** the farm turn **L** down the field edge by the wall signposted *Dartmeet*. Keep the wall to your right. Join a more obvious track and continue downhill, at times technical. Cross the river via a 3rd set of stepping stones. Climb and turn **R** through a gate immediately beyond the house then turn **L** steeply uphill on road.

8 Go past *Pixieland Gift Shop* (nice gnomes!) Cross the cattle grid and turn sharp **R** signposted *Bridlepath to Brimpts Farm*. Go through the farm, past the tearoom, bear **L** then **R** between buildings soon picking up 'Path' signposts as you descend towards the river. Go down a wide smooth track to the field gate by a ruin. Cross the field and go through a bridlegate.

9 Fourth set of stepping stones. Technical rocky challenge with the occasional carry. Cross the clapper bridge, then at the tarmac turn **L**. Follow the road to the farm, turn **R** then bear **L** onto a wide stone and grass track. Shortly at a fork of wide stone tracks bear **R** signposted *Bridlepath*.

10 Technical descent with views of an amazing white house ahead. More stepping stones. Rock-strewn push uphill to complete loop. At the T-junction with the main forest road, turn **R** to rejoin the outward route (go through the gate, past a stone building, over open ground, bear **R** at the fork to go through the bridlegate).

11 At the road you have two choices:

> **OR** **(a)** repeat the outward route in reverse

> **OR** **(b)** turn **L** then **R** and return by road

Warren
House
Inn

6

5

Headland
Warren
Farm

CHALLACOMBE
DOWN

Challacombe

SOUSSONS
WARREN

4

Soussons
Farm

3

**Postbridge &
Challacombe Down**

Directions – Postbridge & Challacombe Down

1 Exit the car park and turn **L** on the *B3212*. Cross the bridge and turn **R** onto the narrow lane signposted *Lydgate House, Bridlepath to Lydgate and Pizwell*. Go past the hotel and continue in the same direction on a track through a gate and into the field.

2 Follow the well-signposted grassy track around the field edge, join a more defined earth and stone track. At one point a stream crosses the path - this is a potential mudbath. Follow the wide track through *Pizwell Farm* and go **SA** onto the track opposite, **ignoring** the tarmac lane to the left. Cross the stream via the ford or stepping stones.

3 At the T-junction with the road turn **R**, then after 500m take the first **L** onto a broad stone track with a blue arrow on a wooden post. At the farm go through the gate, then turn **R** signposted *Challacombe Farm*. Follow signs along the field edge towards the wood then go through the gate in the stone wall to the **R** before reaching the wood. Follow the track round to the **R** and descend to cross the stream.

4 Join a better stone-based track which turns to concrete through *Challacombe Farm*. As the concrete drive swings **R** towards the road, continue **SA** through the gate signposted *Bridlepath*. Follow this fine, gentle grassy track between ferns.

5 After 1.5km, at the outbuildings of *Headland Warren Farm*, bear **L** to go through the farm and through a bridlegate. Climb to a T-junction of tracks and turn **L** signposted *Bridlepath to Warren House Inn*. Continue climbing on a narrow track. Please show courtesy to other path users.

6 Descend. At the T-junction with a broader stone path, just before the ruins and the stream, turn **L** towards the edge of the forest (or continue **SA** uphill for *Warren House Inn*). Go through the gate then shortly bear **R** at a fork of tracks signposted *Bridlepath to County Road near Soussons*. Join the forest road and turn **L**. You can either follow this back to the road (lift your bike over the stile at the end) **OR** use the bridlepath which starts shortly on the **R**, crossing the main forest road and aiming towards the gate and *Soussons Farm* ahead to rejoin the outward route. Whichever route you choose, at the road turn **R**.

7 **Easy to miss:** after 1.5km, having **ignored** a left turn to *Pizwell*, take the next broad stone track to the **L** downhill. Go through the gate and follow the track between buildings onto a green lane. Go through *Merripit Farm* and take the next broad stone track to the **L**. Continue **SA**, then at the T-junction with the *B3212* turn **L** to return to start.

PHOTO: ANDY HEADING

Lustleigh
Cleave

naton

3

Freeland

Kestor
Inn

2

Trendlebere
Down

S **P**

MORETONHAMPSTEAD A382

Leighon

11

10

12

BOVEY
TRACEY

eator
cks

0 miles   1

N

0 km   1

B3387

**Grimspound &
Hound Tor**

Directions – Grimspound & Hound Tor

1 Turn **L** downhill out of the car park, then shortly **L** again sharply back on yourself signposted *Unsuitable for motors*. Go downhill then along the valley bottom, following signs for *Manaton* and **ignoring** a bridge/bridlegate to the right. Cross *Becka Brook* via a ford turn **L** and follow 'Path' signs as the trail zig zags **R** then **L** up through the forestry. Steep climb.

2 At a X-roads of tracks continue **SA** uphill signposted *Bridlepath to Water for Manaton*. Join tarmac as the gradient eases. At a T-junction turn **R** signposted *Bridlepath to Bovey Valley for Lustleigh and Manaton (direct)*. Go past a thatched house and shortly turn **L** just before the next house signposted *Bridlepath*. At a X-roads of tracks turn **L** (there is a private drive to right) then at the next junction of tracks by a corrugated iron garage turn **L** signposted *Bridlepath to Manaton*.

3 Attractive singletrack with some roots and rocks. At the T-junction with the road turn **L**. Vast stones in the wall ahead. At the X-roads turn **R** signposted *Hound Tor, Widecombe*. After 2km take the second **R** onto a no through road signposted *Boddown Farm, Barracott*. The tarmac turns to track signposted *Byway*.

4 **Ignore** a bridleway to the right at the gate. Continue straight ahead. At the T-junction with the road turn **R**, then after about 1.5km turn **L** at a X-roads of minor lanes onto a no through road signposted *Hookner Coombe*. **Ignore** turns to left then right. Go past a house with fridge-sized stones. Exceedingly steep climb on concrete and grass track. As the track swings right towards the house, bear **L** to continue in same direction uphill.

5 The stone track turns to grass through ferns. Long steep climb with ever better views behind. Turn **R** through a gate in the wall, then turn **L** to continue in the same direction, soon reaching the top. Descend to the road and turn **L**

6 Descend on road, then just before a hairpin bend bear **L** onto a stone and grass track climbing towards, then around, the perimeter of *Grimspound* (keep the wall to your left). Climb for 1.2km to the summit - excellent panoramic views over rolling *Devon* patchwork of fields and clumps of woodland with tors on the horizon to the right.

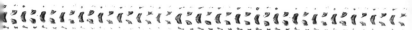

7 Follow towards the **right-hand** end of forest. Superb descent. At the T-junction with the road turn **L** then **R** signposted *Bridlepath to Jay's Grave*. At the road by *Jay's Grave* go **SA** through a gate ahead onto a wide grassy track.

8 Go round the edge of the field through a bridlegate and continue **SA** downhill (ie **not** right on a more obvious track towards the barn). At the road turn **R** then at road junction with a thatched house ahead bear **L.** Shortly at the point where a road joins from the left, go **SA** onto grass towards the right-hand end of *Hound Tor* (there is a blue arrow on wooden post).

9 Climb past *Hound Tor* and aim downhill towards the **left-hand** end of *Greator Rocks* ahead, where rocks meet woodland. Go though the bridlegate just to the **R** of a stack of rocks signposted *Bridlepath to Leighon via Haytor Down*. Testing narrow descent with stone drainage channels. Cross a stone bridge over the stream.

10 Walk and ride through Dingly Dell boulder fields. Emerge at a wooden post and bear **L** signposted *Bridlepath to Leighon*. Go through several gates and follow the track as it turns sharp **R** uphill signposted *County Road below Blackhill*. Steep push, then the track levels out for superb breezy views.

11 At the T-junction with the road turn **R**. After 800m **ignore** a bridlepath to the left just at the edge/start of the wood. Continue climbing then, as the gradient eases, keep an eye out for a signpost *Bridlepath to Haytor Bovey Road near Ullacombe* pointing alongside the wall, bearing **L** away from the road.

12 Superb descent though woodland. At the T-junction with road turn **L**, then **(easy to miss)** on a fast descent take the **third L** - the first two are tarmac drives, the third is a wide stone track signposted *Bridlepath to Manaton Road at Reddaford Water*. At the bottom of this track, at the T-junction with the road, turn **L** for 800m to return to the car park at the start.

PHOTO: ANDY HEADING

PHOTO: ANDY HEADING

Langdon

2

▲
EASDON T⟨

Easdon
Farm

3

N

North Bovey

Ring O'Bells

Dickford Water

Barnecourt

7

River Bovey

Peck
Farm

4

5

Luckdon

6

Langstone
Cottage

Foxworthy
Bridge

Barracott

Manaton

miles

1

1

**North Bovey, Whooping
Rock & Foxworthy**

Directions – North Bovey, Whooping Rock & Foxworthy

1 Turn **L** out of *North Bovey* car park, first **R** at *Fairbrook Bridge* then at the T-junction turn **L** signposted *Manaton*. Steep climb. **Ignore** a right turn to *Moretonhampstead*. **Easy to miss:** keep an eye out for a wide stone track to the **L** signposted *Byway to Langdon and Bridlepath to Easdon*. Fine views across the valley to *Hameldown*.

2 At the junction with tarmac by *Langdon Farm* turn **L**. Steep descent. At the T-junction by white Give Way lines turn **L** then, after 1km, take the first road **L** by *Easdon*. The tarmac turns to track by a cluster of buildings signposted *Byway to Barracott*. Go through a gate, still climbing.

3 Just before the next gate, at the top of the climb, turn **L** uphill signposted *Bridlepath to County Road near Luckdon via Easdon*. The track leads towards the tor then bears **R** to run parallel with the wall. At the corner of the wall **do not** go straight ahead but turn **R** and follow a faint track as it contours around the hillside through fern and gorse. At the next wall corner continue **SA** towards the conifer plantation ahead.

4 **Easy to miss:** after 150m, shortly after passing several low flat boulders to the right, bear **R** downhill through ferns on faint track starting by a small cairn of stones. Go through a bridgegate into the woodland onto a grass then stone track. Continue downhill **ignoring** turns to left and right until reaching a wooden barrier. Shortly turn **R** by firebeaters and a *Bridleway* signpost.

5 Descend a series of drop offs, go through a gate on the **L** and continue down to the road. At the road turn **R** then first **L** by *Langstone Cottage* signposted *Lustleigh*. **Easy to miss:** after 400m on this fast descent turn first **R** signposted *Manaton, Unsuitable for wide vehicles*. Descend then climb. On a sharp right-hand bend bear **L** (in effect go **SA**) signposted *Bridlepath to Foxworthy Bridge*.

6 At the bottom of the descent, on a concrete and grass track, just before a gate and a 'Private' sign, turn **R** onto a narrow track signposted 'Path'. Rejoin the concrete track and turn **R**. Shortly fork **L** signposted *Bridlepath for Peck Farm and road near Barnecourt* and go past a large thatched house. Climb, go through the gate and turn **L** onto a concrete track.

7 At the T-junction with the road turn **R** then, shortly after the brow of the hill, turn **L** just before the buildings onto a no through road. The tarmac turns to track. At a signpost for *North Bovey Village* you have a choice - turn **L** for the ford/stepping stones signposted *Byway to Manaton Road*, then turn **R** to return to the car park ▶OR go **SA** into the village, and keep bearing **L** to return to same point. Now, do you want to wash your bike?

PHOTO: ANDY HEADING

PHOTO: ANDY HEADING

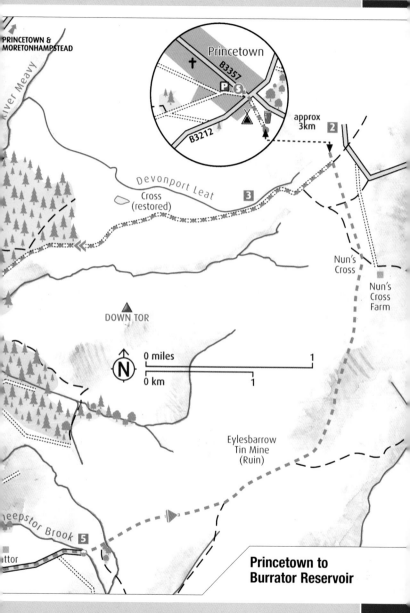

PRINCETOWN & MORETONHAMPSTEAD

River Meavy

Princetown

B3357

P

approx 3km

B3212

2

Devonport Leat

Cross (restored)

3

Nun's Cross

Nun's Cross Farm

DOWN TOR

0 miles 1

N

0 km 1

Eylesbarrow Tin Mine (Ruin)

Sheepstor Brook

5

...ttor

Princetown to Burrator Reservoir

N

0 miles   1

0 km   1

River Av

P 3
Shipley Bridge

Didworthy

Lutton

South Brent

2

Higher Lutton

Bloody
Pool

B3372

A38 (1)

Avon Dam & Scorriton

Directions – Avon Dam & Scorriton

1   Turn **R** out of *South Brent* car park. At the T-junction turn **R**, cross the railway bridge then bear **L** signposted *2 ton weight limit*. After 400m take the first road **R** signposted *Lutton*. Climb steeply, then steadily. After almost 800m turn **L** downhill onto a lane by a triangle of grass, shortly bearing **R** onto a broad stone track signposted *Bridlepath to Didworthy*.

2   Cross the ford, go through a gate, climb steeply then steadily as the track narrows, passing through two bridlegates. Climb to the summit, shortly go through a third gate then, at the tarmac by *Pinewood Lodge*, turn **R** downhill. At the T-junction turn **L**, cross the river then at the next T-junction turn **R** signposted *Shipley Bridge* onto a no through road.

3   Immediately after the car park but **before** the bridge turn **L** onto a tarmac lane signposted *Brockhill Ford* (*Abbot's Way*). After 1.2km cross the stream, leave the woodland and emerge onto open moorland. About 1.2km after the stream crossing, with the dam now in sight, on a sweeping left-hand bend by a passing place, bear **R** onto a broad grass and stone track climbing away from the road up to the dam.

4   The track is rougher and ill-defined after the dam. At the first 'corner' of the reservoir, bear **R** away from the water - then after 200m at the junction with a wider, more defined grassy track coming from the left, turn **R** uphill (this is *Abbot's Way*). Pass to the **L** of a small plantation and go through a bridlegate signposted *Abbot's Way*.

5   Tricky little descent to cross the stream, then immediately fork **L** (blue arrow). The wonderful grassy descent becomes a narrow track down into woodland. Go through two gates by Lord of the Rings beech trees and roots. Follow signpost for *Cross Furzes**. Cross the stream via the clapper bridge or the ford. Steep broad, stony climb.

* ▶OR▷ for a short cut turn **R** signposted *Moor Cross, South Brent*.
      Rejoin at instruction N° 9.

6   At the X-roads at the top turn **L** signposted *Combe, Scorriton, Hayford Hall*. After 400m fork **L** signposted *Hayford Hall*. At the end of the tarmac go **SA** onto a wide stone track. Go through the gate onto the moor signposted *Bridlepath to Scorriton via Chalk Ford*. Bear **R** following the direction of the signpost for 200m to the wall corner (ie do **not** take more obvious stone track to the left). Soon cross the stream.

7   There are lots of tracks on the ground not marked on the map. Aim to bear **R** and descend steeply on a grass and stone track to arrive at a narrow wooden bridge over the stream. After a short climb this becomes a long fast descent on a broad loose stone track. Join tarmac, then at the T-junction in *Scorriton* turn **R** (or turn **L** for *Tradesman's Arms* PH). Shortly, on a sharp left-hand bend turn **R** signposted *Lower Coombe, Higher Coombe*.

8   Descend, cross the stream and climb, **ignoring** turns to left and right. Steep climb. Rejoin the outward route. **Ignore** a right turn to *Hayford Hall* then opposite a left turn to *Buckfast* turn **R** downhill on a broad stone track.

9   Steep descent, cross the stream, turn **L** signposted *Bridlepath to Moor Cross for South Brent*. Steep then steady climb to emerge on the moor. Follow this grassy track running parallel with a wall to the left - fantastic views. At the corner, continue in the same direction, passing through two closely spaced gates with blue paint splashes. Almost immediately, turn **R** through a field gate and go down across the field bearing slightly away from the fence on the left to aim for a gate and signpost in the fence ahead at the bottom of the field.

10   Follow the direction of the signpost diagonally **R** across the field to the far corner to find a hidden bridlegate. Go through the gate and turn **L**. Emerge at the road, bear **R** then take the first road **R** by a triangle of grass. Descend then final climb. At the T-junction by *Bloody Pool Cross*, turn **R** signposted *Shipley Bridge* then shortly **L** signposted *Lutton*. Fast descent. At the T-junction at the bottom turn **L** to return to *South Brent*.

LYDFORD TO MARY TAVY

GRADE:

DISTANCE: 17KM

TOTAL ASCENT: 256M

START/FINISH: LYDFORD

GRID REFERENCE: 501833

PARKING: LYDFORD FALLS CAR PARK

CAFÉ: BRING SANDWICHES

PUBLIC HOUSE: CASTLE INN LYDFORD Tel: 01822 820 241 or ELEPHANT'S NEST, HORNDON Tel: 01822 810 273
or PETER TAVY INN Tel: 01822 810 348

EARLY MORNING SUNSHINE ON DARTMOOR **PHOTO:** *ANDY HEADING*

Lydford to Mary Tavy – Dartmoor

Introduction

One of the easier **Dartmoor** rides with nothing too challenging and two excellent pubs along the way – save this ride as a treat for yourselves when you just want a gentle potter.

The ride

The first sight of the moor at the end of the track leading up from *Lydford Gorge* car park may have you scratching your heads *'Where does the path go?'*. This is the only time on the whole ride where this will happen - at the top of the ridge ahead is the main *A386* and once you are across that it is all plain sailing. Great tracks and views east into the heart of the moor, a descent to cross the *River Tavy* at *Hill Bridge*, a short climb, an easy glide down to the *Peter Tavy Inn* and more good stone tracks to recross the *Tavy* on your way to *Mary Tavy*. The final hill, part on road and part offroad on grassy tracks is rewarded with wide views to the curious little church on top of **Brentor**, a swooping grassy descent to the road and an easy run back to the start, with the odd splash just to prove you've been out.

Making a day of it

Firing ranges permitting *(see page 13)* link this ride to the *Peter Tavy & Merrivale* ride at GR 533801 ie cross *Hill Bridge* and turn left towards **Wapsworthy** and **Baggator**. Alternatively, to the north, a short road section will take you to **Lydford** and the start of the *Granite Way* which links to the *Meldon Reservoir* ride. A third option is a there-and-back ride, climbing to 550m, following the stone-based old tramway starting from the *Fox & Hounds* PH at **Shortacombe** up onto the moor beneath *Great Links Tor*. Start a GR 525866, head north to the hairpin at GR 546887 and turn around at the top at GR 5

PHOTO: ANDY HEADING

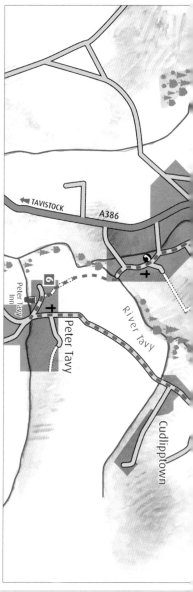

TAVISTOCK ← A386

Peter Tavy Inn

6

Peter Tavy

River Tavy

Cudlipptown

North
Brentor

Lydford
Falls

Mary Tavy

GIBBET HILL

8

P
6

2

N

0 km

0 miles

3 A386

OKEHAMPTON

P

Elephant's
Nest

Horndon

4

MERRIVALE RANGE

5

Lydford to Mary Tavy

Directions – Lydford to Mary Tavy

1 Exit *Lydford Falls* car park, turn **L** towards *Lydford Village* to cross the bridge and immediately turn **R** (tricky crossing on blind bend - **take care!**) onto a broad stone track, taking the **left-hand** fork signposted *Bridlepath*. Climb and follow the track round to the **L** to its end.

2 Go through the field gate with a *West Devon Way* sticker and turn **R** after the first telegraph pole towards the steep slope up to your right and the obvious telegraph pole in a second line of poles. The track becomes more defined. Immediately after crossing a stone water channel across the path leave the stone path and fork **R** onto a wide grassy track.

3 Cross the main *A386* via two field gates to join the wide stone track opposite signposted *Bridleway* (blue waymark). Follow this ever better stone track. At the T-junction with a wide gravel road with a walled embankment ahead turn **R**. Go past a squat grey building, continuing on the main track, soon descending. At the road turn **L** (or for the *Elephant's Nest* PH in *Horndon* turn **R**) then shortly first **R** signposted *Lower Creason*.

4 The tarmac turns to track and swings **L**, signposted *Bridleway to Hill Bridge*. Go past one farm, cross a bridge and go through a second farm and several gates. At the road bear **R** downhill. Cross the bridge and climb steeply. At the T-junction turn **R**, signposted *Peter Tavy*. for link to the *Merrivale ride* turn **L**.

5 Good long easy tarmac descent. Immediately after the church in *Peter Tavy* turn **R** by *Gatehouse Barn* towards the *Peter Tavy Inn*. Bear **L** onto the lower track by the pub car park then shortly take the first track to the **R** signposted *Bridleway to Mary Tavy*.

6 Fine track. Cross the river, go past *Mary Tavy church* then at the T-junction turn **R** signposted *Horndon*. **Ignore** a right turn towards *Horndon*. Cross the bridge, start climbing then on a right-hand bend by Glebe Cottage turn **L** uphill onto a wide stone track.

7 At the X-roads with the *A386* go **SA** signposted *Brentor* (**take care** - poor visibility). Cross the cattlegrid and take the first wide stone track to the **R**, soon forking **L** onto a wide grassy track signposted *West Devon Way* (blue arrow). Climb then enjoy a superb grassy descent with good views. At the T-junction with the road bear **R** then shortly, on a sharp left-hand bend, bear **R** onto a stone and grass track signposted *Bridleway, West Devon Way.*

8 **Easy to miss:** after 800m, with the house ahead about 300m away, bear **R** onto a parallel grassy track. Follow in the same direction alongside the wall and fence to the house with a wooden garden shed to rejoin the outward route. Turn sharp **L** through a wooden field gate, descend to the road and turn **L** to return to the start.

PHOTO: ANDY HEADING

Exmoor

Square mile for square mile Exmoor is surely the best National Park in Britain for mountain biking - can anywhere else boast such a quantity, quality and variety of trails? Routes up on the cliff tops with views across the Bristol Channel to Wales; intimate wooded coombes with twisting testing rooty singletrack; remote moorland that could easily be compared to that in the Peak District or further north; and then there is the speciality of the region - rollercoaster bedrock descents with enough drop-offs to test the keenest mountain biker; there really is something to suit every taste.

Exmoor

sponsored by

www.endura.co.uk

Twelve rides are described on **Exmoor** and it would not be impossible to find twelve more, such is the quantity of well-maintained bridleways, byways and RUPPs (Roads Used as Public Paths). The rides in the north are dominated by the coastal views: from **Lynton** and the **Valley of Rocks** in the west through to **Selworthy Beacon** in the east, the tracks take you high along the cliffs with wonderful coastal views. The central rides touch on rough and rugged moorland; some of these rides are best savoured as experiences of raw elemental nature, not as a challenge to break personal best times. They are a chance to blast away cobwebs and the occasional wind-battered tree will show how effectively that will happen.

The principal villages of central and southern **Exmoor** – **Exford, Winsford, Simonsbath, Withypool, Dulverton** and **Wheddon Cross** can all be linked together by interlocking rides enabling you to do two, three or even more routes in a day if the conditions are right and you are feeling fit and up for it. **Porlock** is the other obvious centre to the north of the region with several rides nearby and easy access to almost all of the moor.

No times have been given for the routes as strong winds, rain and soft conditions underfoot can easily double the effort for any given ride if done on a stormy day in winter as compared to a dry dusty day in summer.

Dunkery Beacon and Tarr Steps
The National Park has specifically requested us not to promote rides in these two areas, in order to avoid exacerbating user conflict. They are very popular with walkers – and as there are so many bridleway alternatives in the park, the request does not seem unreasonable. Think of them in the same light as the voluntary restrictions on **Snowdon**: you have every legal right to use the bridleways in the area but try to avoid times that are busy, particularly summer weekends.

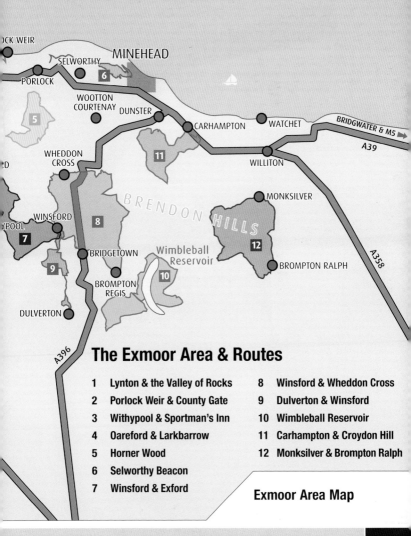

The Exmoor Area & Routes

1. Lynton & the Valley of Rocks
2. Porlock Weir & County Gate
3. Withypool & Sportman's Inn
4. Oareford & Larkbarrow
5. Horner Wood
6. Selworthy Beacon
7. Winsford & Exford
8. Winsford & Wheddon Cross
9. Dulverton & Winsford
10. Wimbleball Reservoir
11. Carhampton & Croydon Hill
12. Monksilver & Brompton Ralph

Exmoor Area Map

LYNTON

A39   MINEHEAD

P

e Valley
Rocks

PO

S

Bridge
Inn

B3234

Lyn Bridge
(FB)

FB

8

West Lyn
Farmhouse

A39

B3223

East
erton

Cattle
Grid

Scoresdown

7

SIMONSBATH

Cheriton

Sparhanger Cross

South
Sparhanger

6

5

Radsbury

0 miles   1

N

0 km   1

**Lynton & the
Valley of Rocks**

Directions – Lynton &
the Valley of Rocks

1 Exit Bottom Meadow car park and turn **L** following the main road through *Lynton* past shops and the *Post Office* towards the *Valley of Rocks*. Go through the *Valley of Rocks* then opposite the gate tower for *Lee Abbey* (down to your right) turn **L** through a gate onto a track signposted *Bridleway to Six Acre Cross*. Fabulous sea cliff views. After 400m turn **L** sharply back on yourself - same sign, there is a footpath ahead.

2 Superb climbing track. Another zigzag, all well signposted. Go through a farm onto tarmac. At the T-junction with the road turn **R** (by a caravan park). At the next T-junction turn **R** signposted *Caffyn's Farm*.

3 After 2.4km at a X-roads of lanes (not your priority) take the 1st road **L** signposted *Parracombe*. At the offset X-roads with the *A39* at *Martinhoe Cross* turn **L** then **R** signposted *Woolhanger*. The tarmac ends, follow the main track down through the farm, on an ever more stony surface. **Easy to miss:** at a fork of tracks near to a detached house, 200m after passing the estate office on your left, bear **R** then sharp **L** signposted *Permitted Bridleway to West Ilkerton*. (Ie do **not** cross the stream).

4 Fine fast concrete then stone track. Cross a small river then climb steeply. At *West Ilkerton Farm* turn **L** on tarmac to continue climbing. At the T-junction with the road near *East Ilkerton* amid grey stone buildings turn **R**. Climb steeply then more gently. Cross the cattle grid and immediately bear **L** onto a grass and stone track running alongside the wall to the left signposted *Bridleway to Radsbury*.

5 After 500m at a X-roads of tracks by a wooden post turn **L** through a gate onto a sunken track signposted *Sparhanger Cross via South Sparhanger*. At the tarmac bear **L** downhill (Radsbury is to the right). Descend steeply, cross the concrete-bottomed ford then climb steeply through the farm. At the T-junction turn **R** (GR 719463).

6   Shortly, on a sharp right-hand bend, bear **L** signposted *Bridleway to Cheriton*. At a gate go **SA** across the field (same sign). This soon becomes an obvious track. At the end of the field follow a loose stone track down to a ford/bridge. Very steep stony climb. At the T-junction with the road turn **L** signposted *Scoresdown, Lyndown*.

7   Steep descent on what used to be a tarmac road. Climb steeply. At the X-roads with the A39 go **SA** signposted *West Lyn*. Views to *Wales* ahead. After 600m, on a sharp left-hand bend by *West Lyn Farmhouse* turn **R** then **L** between the wall and the barn, signposted *Lynbridge*.

8   Great descent! At the T-junction at the bottom turn **L** then **R** to cross the bridge and emerge by the *Bridge Inn*. Bear **R** by the pub then turn **R** downhill on the road and continue **SA** signposted *Lynton, Valley of Rocks* to return to the car park at the start.

PHOTO: ANDY HEADING

PHOTO: ANDY HEADING

PHOTO: ANDY HEADING

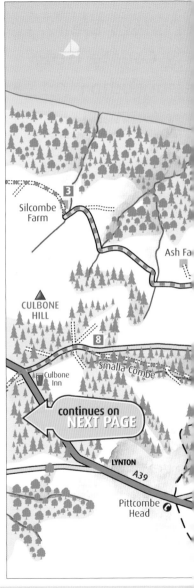

Silcombe Farm

3

Ash Fa

▲ CULBONE HILL

8

Culbone Inn

Smalla Combe

continues on NEXT PAGE

LYNTON

A39

Pittcombe Head

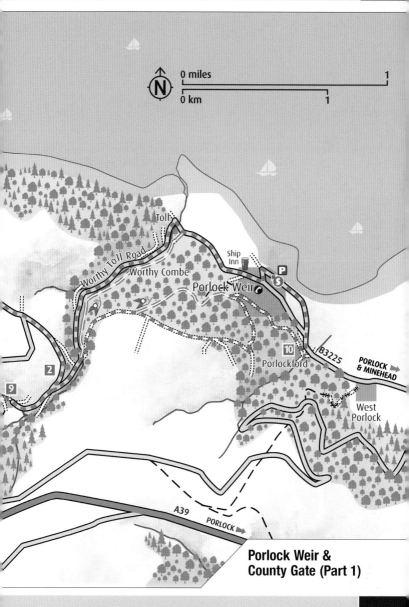

0 miles 1
0 km 1

Toll

Worthy Toll Road

Worthy Combe

Ship Inn

Porlock Weir

P
S

10

B3225

Porlockford

PORLOCK & MINEHEAD ▶

2

9

West Porlock

A39 **PORLOCK** ▶

**Porlock Weir &
County Gate (Part 1)**

PHOTO: ANDY HEADING

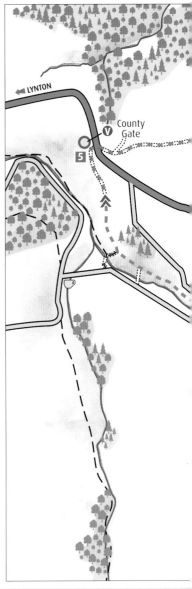

County Gate

◄ LYNTON

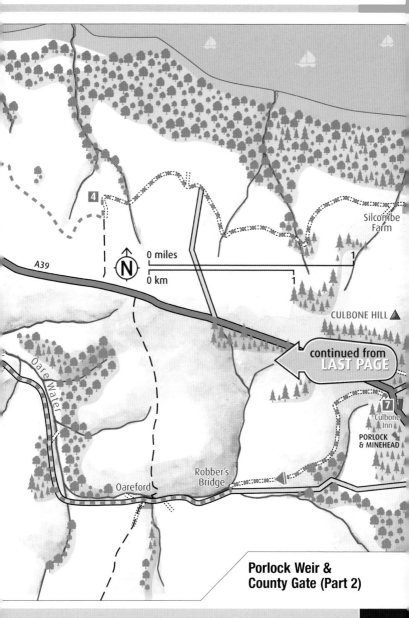

**Porlock Weir &
County Gate (Part 2)**

A39

Silcombe
Farm

4

0 miles   1

(N)

0 km   1

CULBONE HILL ▲

continued from
LAST PAGE

7

Culbone
Inn

**PORLOCK
& MINEHEAD**

Oare Water

Robber's
Bridge

Oareford

Directions – Porlock Weir & County Gate

1 From the main car park in *Porlock Weir* cross the road onto the minor lane between the *Ship Inn* and *Andrews on the Weir* Restaurant. Climb steeply then at the T-junction turn **R** signposted *Worthy, Ashley Combe*. Go through* the toll gate and climb steeply.

> * for an alternative, steep offroad climb, about 100m **before** the toll gate there is a bridlepath to the **L** that runs parallel with the toll road. This joins the toll road higher up.

2 Follow the road round a sharp **right-hand** hairpin bend signposted *Countisbury, Lynmouth*. At a junction of roads and tracks continue **SA** uphill on a lane signposted *Ash Farm* (ie **NOT** *Yarner Farm* to the right nor *Countisbury* to the left).

3 The tarmac turns to track after *Silcombe Farm*. The good stone track turns to mainly grass over a stone base. At the junction with road beyond a gate go **SA** signposted *Bridleway to County Gate*. Go through a gate into an open field by a 4-way wooden post and turn **L** uphill signposted *Bridleway to Oareford, County Gate*.

4 Climb very steeply along the **left-hand** field edge, go through a bridlegate and turn **R** parallel with the wall to the right. Stay on the lower faint track close to the wall on the right. Emerge at the road by a white house, cross **SA** onto a track opposite signposted *Bridleway*.

5 Cross the main road near to the visitor centre, going through a field gate marked *Bridleway* onto a grassy track. Follow close to the fence on the left to join a more defined path, descending steeply. At the bottom of the hill bear **L*** through a bridlegate signposted *Oare Church*. Go through several gates.

> * for refreshments bear **R** to continue downhill to the road and turn **L** along the road to *The Buttery Tearoom*.

6   At the road bear **R**. Cross the bridge and turn **L** signposted *Oareford, Robber's Bridge*. After 3km cross *Robber's Bridge* over the river (GR 820464) and turn immediately **L** uphill onto an obvious track signposted *Bridleway to Culbone Inn*.

7   At the top go through a gate into the *Culbone Inn* car park. Cross the main A39 (do this near to the car park - there is better visibility here) onto the minor lane opposite signposted *Culbone Church*.

8   **Easy to miss:** shortly after passing a road to the left signposted *Permitted footpath to Silcombe* turn **R** through a gate onto a downhill track through pine woodland. Cross the bridge to the other side of the valley and bear **L** to continue downhill on a forest track.

9   At a junction by a 3-way wooden post with a house ahead turn **L** signposted *Porlock Weir*. Briefly rejoin the outward route on the hairpin bend. Bear **R** downhill then **easy to miss:** after 250m bear **R** through a gate by a *Public Path to Porlock Weir* signpost.

     ▶**OR** In addition to the route described below there are two other, more technical, bridleway descents possible, both dropping down to the *Porlock Weir* road: the first starts on the **L** as soon as you leave tarmac and runs parallel with the toll road, the second comes after a further 400m, also to the **L**.

10   Short climb. Follow the red-tipped waymarks and signs for *Porlock Ford*. At a T-junction of tracks turn **L**. At the T-junction with the road turn **L** to return to the *Ship Inn, Porlock Weir*.

PHOTO: NICK COTTON

Horsen Farm

4

5

Sherdon Farm

Sherdon W

Sherdon Bridge

Sherdon Cottage

Sportsman's Inn

6

Litton Water

Mudgate Cross

◄ NORTH MOLTON

PHOTO: ANDY HEADING

EXFORD

2

3 River Barle

Withypool ✝

P · S

WINSFORD & DULVERTON

Withypool Common

Porchester's
Post

ⓝ

0 miles   1

0 km   1

ool

Upper Willingford
Bridge

Cattle grid

**Withypool &
the Sportsman's Inn**

Directions – Withypool & the Sportsman's Inn

1 Exit the *Withypool* car park and turn **L**. Cross the bridge, go through the village and turn **L** immediately before the *Royal Oak* PH. After 200m take the first **L** onto a no through road signposted *Westerclose*. Steady climb on tarmac which turns to track at the gate. Go **SA** at the road onto a continuation of the track.

2 At a fork of tracks bear **L** signposted *Bridleway to Picked Stones & Horsen Ford*. There are many tracks on the ground not marked on the map. At the next fork bear **R** on the upper track (the lower track leads into a field) then at the 3rd fork by a wooden post bear **L** signposted *Simonsbath via Cow Castle*.

3 Superb grassy descent with magnificent views over heather and down through valleys. Go down through several gates into woodland to join a fine broad stone track past *Lord of the Rings* style roots and trees then a small coniferous plantation. At the ford continue on the same side of the river for 50m to cross via a bridge. Cross a 2nd footbridge, following the main track up and away from the river. Climb alongside a line of trees then enter an enclosed canopy of trees.

4 At the road turn **L** then almost immediately **L** again through double gates onto a new stone track. At the next gate follow the obvious grassy track diagonally **L** across the field to another gate. Climb to and go through a 3rd gate. Go over the brow of the hill and descend on an obvious track to double gates (all, presently, with blue rope and catches). Good views ahead.

5 Follow the **left-hand** field edge through two fields then at a T-junction with a broad, enclosed track turn **L** signposted *Bridleway to Sherdon*. Go past the remote house at *Sherdon*. Descend on a lovely track to cross the river then climb. At the T-junction with the road turn **R** then shortly, at *Withypool Cross*, turn **R** again signposted *North & South Molton*.

6   Go past the *Sportsman's Inn* then take the 1st road **L** signposted *Twitchen, Molland*. At *Mudgate Cross* turn 1st **L** at the X-roads of lanes signposted *Molland, Hawkridge*. Fast descent. At the junction by a cattlegrid turn **L** onto a broad stone track. Descend to cross *Upper Willingford Bridge* then climb. The track becomes rougher after *Porchester Post*. At the T-junction with the road bear **R** onto a track signposted *Withypool Contour Track*. At the road turn **L** to return to the start.

PHOTO: ANDY HEADING

N

0 miles 1
0 km 1

Larkbarrow
Ruins

3

Alderman's
Barrow

4

2

Almsworthy
Common

EXFORD

Cattle Grid

Oareford & Larkbarrow

PHOTO: ANDY HEADING

PHOTO: ANDY HEADING

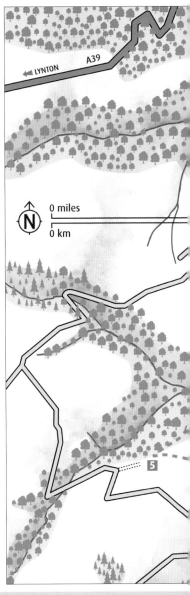

Porlock

West
Luccombe

2

A39

MINEHEAD ▶

Packhorse
Bridge

Horner

S **P**

Flora's Ride (Track)

3

Horner
Wood

Luccombe

4

FB ◀◀

Webber's
Post

7 ➡

6

Cloutsham

Dunkery & Horner Wood
(Nature Reserve)

Horner Wood

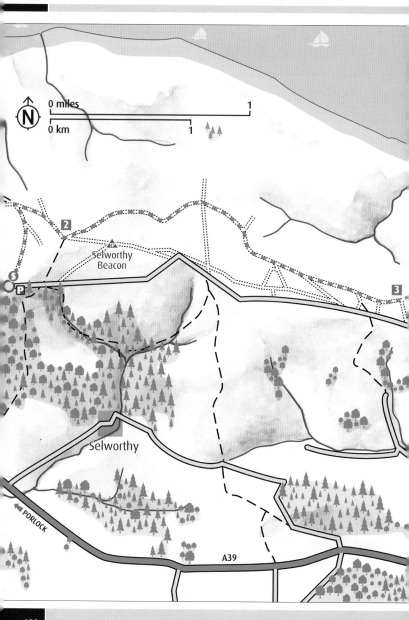

Selworthy
Beacon

Selworthy

PORLOCK

A39

Red Lion Pub

Higher Town

Harbour

Wood Combe

Higher Town

Minehead

M5 →

Selworthy Beacon

Directions – Selworthy Beacon

1 From the right-hand edge of the gravel parking area take the track by the low wooden *Hurlestone Point* signpost, aiming northwest. At the fork of tracks bear **L** (no sign). At the T-junction with a similar broad stone track with an acorn post to your right, turn sharp **R** uphill.

2 At a fork bear **L** on the lower path signposted *Coast Path*. Huge views west to dramatic cliffs, north to *Wales*, east to the island of *Flat Holm*. Fork **L** staying on the track parallel with road. At the tarmac lane (GR 926484) go **SA**.

3 After almost 1km, bear **L** off the main 'tractor' track onto a narrower path. Follow this path on a mixture of surfaces. After a climb then a descent, at a 5-way post by a wooden bench, bear **L** signposted *Minehead Seafront*.

4 Superb descending track with great views. Go past a square concrete parking area then past a low concrete building to the left. At a grassy T-junction turn **L** to continue downhill (no sign). At a multi-junction of paths by a 4-way post with a red-tiled house ahead turn sharp **L** downhill signposted *Minehead Harbour*.

5 Join a better stone (vehicle) track and turn sharp **R** then almost immediately sharply **L** just after a wooden barrier to continue steeply downhill. At the next similar junction turn **R** on a downhill zig zag track by a bench and a (broken) signpost.

6 Emerge at the roundabout on the seafront. Go past the *Old Ship Aground* PH, cafes, harbour and the *'Hands'* sculpture holding a map which marks the start of the *South West Coast Path*. Take the 1st road on the **R** after the *Red Lion* PH signposted *Town Centre, Hospital, Blenheim Gardens* onto Blenheim Road. Shortly, at a 5-way junction of roads, bear **R** onto a narrow street running to the left of a tall, red stone wall.

7 Go up the steps at the end of lane and turn **R** uphill on a broad road to go past *Wyndcott Hotel* and round a sharp left-hand hairpin bend. Go past the church, around a long sweeping left-hand bend then a sharper right-hand bend. Immediately after the cattle grid, before the gradient steepens further, turn **L** signposted *Bridleway, no vehicles*. Shortly, **ignore** a tarmac path to the left then, at a fork, bear **R** on the upper track.

8 At a junction of tracks by a small (water company) building bear **L** to pass close to the compound fence on a contouring track. Superb views down into the wooded combe to the left.

9 At a T-junction of tracks bear **L** downhill then shortly fork **R** for a very steep 400m push on grass to the road. Turn **R** then **L** through the car parking area to rejoin the outward route at a 5-way signpost. Turn **L** and follow *Coast Path* signs, passing through several bridlegates. With cliffs ahead in sight, turn **L** at an acorn sign onto a broad stone and grass track that leads back to the car park at the start (you have missed this turn if you find yourself descending steeply westwards off the edge of Bossington Hill). If you do turn off too soon then you will only come to the minor road leading west back to the start, so it's no big deal.

PHOTO: ANDY HEADING

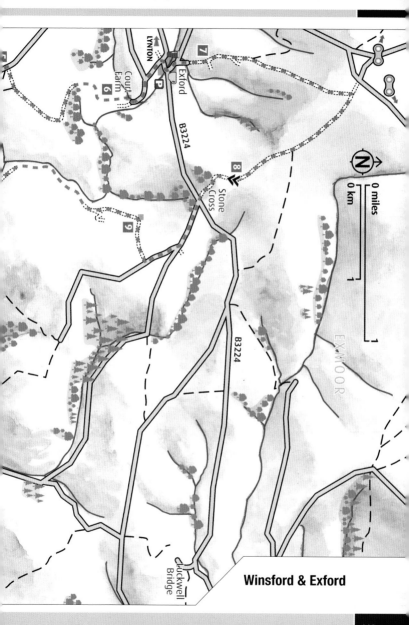

Winsford & Exford

Directions – Winsford & Exford

1 From the centre of *Winsford* go past the *Royal Oak* PH. Climb steeply. Immediately after the cattle grid and the entrance for *Halse Farm* on the left bear **R** uphill away from the road on a broad grass track signposted *Bridleway to Wambarrow*.

2 Many tracks, few shown on the map. Continue climbing on the main track, bearing **L** away from the woodland on the right and soon following the edge of a deep gully (*the Punchbowl*). Towards the end of the *Punchbowl* keep bearing **L** aiming southwest to the road. At the road turn **L** for 300m then, **easy to miss:** shortly after a grassy parking area on the right turn **R** by a low wooden *No Vehicles* signpost. (You may strike lucky and emerge at the road directly opposite this post!)

3 Follow a good track southwest away from the road. There is one rough part in the middle of the descent to *Knaplock*. Continue in the same direction as the field edge becomes a stone track. At the T-junction with a concrete track turn **R**. At the T-junction by the 1st farm (*Higher Knaplock*) turn **R** signposted *Bridleway to Tarr Steps* then at the 2nd farm (*Knaplock*) turn **R** again signposted *Withypool via Comers Gate*. Go through the farm and a gateway then turn **L** on the lower track.

4 Follow the enclosed track and blue paint waymarks. The stream bed/stone-based track turns to a grassy track and passes to the **L** of a line of trees. Follow signs for *Bridleway avoiding bog* on a rough track. Join tarmac near to a farm. At the T-junction with the *B3223* by a cattlegrid turn **L**.

5 Climb to the brow. About 100m after passing a large gravel parking area on the left take the next gate to the **R** signposted *Bridleway to Exford*. Follow the **left-hand** field edge through several gates then at 3-way wooden post after a steep grassy descent turn **L** signposted *Bridleway* through gates and across a level field. Good testing stone descent with drop-offs then a muddy track.

6 Descend to *Court Farm*. Continue in the same direction, climbing gently on tarmac then at the T-junction with the road turn **R** downhill. At the bottom of the hill turn **R** onto the *B3224* into *Exford*, cross the bridge over the *River Exe*, turn **L** by the *Crown Hotel / Exmoor Stores* then 1st **R** onto *Coombe Lane*.

7 Climb steeply, ignoring right turns. The tarmac turns to track and continues to climb. Keep following *Bridleway* signs and blue waymarks. At a T-junction with a wide stone track (by a post with *Dunkery* signposted to the left) turn **R** downhill. Follow the main stone-based track across moorland. Go past a large granite memorial stone and through a gate onto an enclosed track.

8 Fine rollercoaster bedrock stream bed. Push button gates to exit onto the road! At the X-roads with the *B3224* go **SA** signposted *Winsford, Dulverton*. Take the 1st road to the **R** (no sign). After 400m turn **R** onto a stone track by a *Bridleway to Nethercote & Lyncombe* signpost.

9 At the bottom of a steep concrete section turn **L** by a house on your left, soon passing a *Winsford via valley path* signpost. Lots of mud. Some bumpy field sections. One very muddy stretch just before the houses at *West Nethercote*. Go through several gates then enjoy an easy riverside stretch on a broad stone and gravel track. At the T-junction with the road turn **R** and follow it for 2km back to the start.

PHOTO: ANDY HEADING

Kersham Ford

Putham Ford

TP

8

B3224

Wireless Station

EXMOOR NATIONAL PARK

N

0 miles 1
0 km 1

B3224

9

TAUNTON

continues on NEXT PAGE

Goosemoor Cottage

Winsford to Wheddon Cross (Part 1)

TIVERTON

continued from LAST PAGE

Combeshead
Farm

13

Combeshead
Cross

Pulham River

King's Brompton
Farm

10

12
PO

11

Brompton
Regis

Wimbleball
Lake

**Winsford to Wheddon
Cross (Part 2)**

Directions – Winsford to Wheddon Cross

1 From the car park in the centre of *Winsford* follow signs for *Exford* and *Simonsbath*. Towards the end of the village take the first road uphill to the **R** opposite a white house with a tall wall.

2 At the top of the steep climb turn **L** on a broad track by a barn for *East Nurcott Farm*, signposted *Bridleway to Luckwell Bridge via Oldrey Cross*. Climb then descend. At the road bear **R**.

3 At the X-roads with a lane go **SA** onto a track signposted *RUPP to Luckwell Bridge*. A bit muddy though firm underwheel then enjoy the excellent stone rollercoaster descent. At the T-junction at the bottom turn **R** onto tarmac.

4 At the bottom of the hill just before a hump-backed bridge turn **R** onto a stone track signposted *Bridleway to Wheddon Cross*. At the fork of tracks take the upper **right-hand** track signposted *Alternative path avoiding yard*. Cross the bridge over the river and follow round to the **R** to join a sunken, climbing track.

5 At the end of the enclosed track follow the left-hand field edge to a gate into a car park. Cross this to a second gate to pass around the edge of the playing field ahead and through the main *Wheddon Cross* car park.

6 At the X-roads in the centre of *Wheddon Cross* turn **L** on the *A396* towards *Dunster*, then 1st **R** onto no through road signposted *Cutcombe only*, then shortly **R** again signposted *Putham*. On a sharp left-hand bend bear **R** onto a no through road signposted *RUPP to Luxborough via Putham Ford*.

7 Just before the cattlegrid bear **L** onto a wide, muddy stone track signposted *RUPP to Kersham*. At a fork of tracks bear **R**. Fantastic rollercoaster stone track descent. Cross the stream and climb steeply. The gradient eases and you go past a farm. At the road turn **R**. Climb for 2.4km. **Easy to miss:** just after the brow of the hill turn **L** through a metal field gate (blue waymark) by a small gravel area at the side of the road (GR 944373). Go diagonally **L** across the field towards the gate on the horizon.

8 Continue through several gates with blue waymarks, passing to the **L** of the trig point, alongside a fence on your right, then aim diagonally **R** across the field towards the **left-hand** end of the cluster of buildings ahead. Go through a final gate in the hedgerow onto a forest road and continue **SA**.

9 Cross the *B3224* onto the road opposite, signposted *Brompton Regis, Dulverton*. After passing *Goosemoor Cottage* on your right, take the first broad stone track to the **L** signposted *Bridleway to Brompton Regis*.

10 As the main track swings left continue **SA** through a metal gate onto a wide grassy track. Wonderful grassy descent ends at overgrown, muddy section by gate and woodland near *King's Brompton Farm*. Continue in the same direction to emerge at the road and bear **R**.

11 **Easy to miss:** on a sharp left-hand bend at the bottom of a fast tarmac descent (GR 957314) turn **R** onto a track. With a farm ahead turn **L** downhill, cross the stream via the bridge or ford. At the road turn **R**.

12 After the *Post Office* and *church* in *Brompton Regis* turn **R** signposted *Unsuitable for motors*. Steep climb. At *Combeshead Cross* turn **R** signposted *Wheddon Cross, Minehead* then shortly take the first lane to the **L** signposted *Exton, Bridgetown*.

13 Go through the farmyard and a gate set between walls. Descend along the **right-hand** field edge aiming for a bridlegate tucked into the **right-hand** corner. Short overgrown section to cross a wooden bridge and climb to a second bridlegate. Turn **L** between some barns on the right and the farm on the left. Climb on a good stone track.

14 At a X-roads of bridleways go **SA** through a metal gate along the left-hand field edge. At the end of the field take the **left-hand** of two gates (blue waymark). After 100m bear **R** through a bridlegate steeply diagonally downhill across the field to a field gate with a blue waymark. Continue in the same direction past an oak tree to another blue waymarked gate into the woodland.

15 At the X-roads with a major forest track go **SA** (blue waymark). Continue downhill past a house on the left onto a narrow muddy track. Emerge at the road at *Badgers Holt* PH. Turn **R** on the *A396* then 1st **L*** onto *Week Lane* (a no through road) by *Chapel Cottage*.

    * OR If it has been particularly wet, stay on the *A396* for about 1km and take the next road to the left and follow this back to *Winsford*.

16 Cross the hump-backed bridge over the river then turn **R** on a broad stone track signposted *Bridleway to Coppleham*. This section can become very wet and churned up. At the road turn **L** to return to *Winsford*.

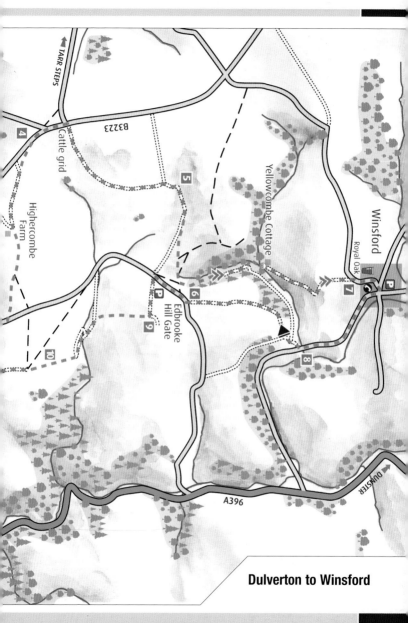

Dulverton to Winsford

Directions – Dulverton to Winsford

1 From the *Lion Hotel* in the centre of *Dulverton* take the *B3223* towards *Lynton* and *Exford*. **Easy to miss:** after 1.6km bear **R** onto a no through road by a house sign for Sweetoaks signposted *RUPP to Court Down*. Shortly fork **R** (ie do NOT go over the cattlegrid). Climb on a stone-based vehicle track with a canopy of trees overhead.

2 At a T-junction of tracks at the top of the climb turn **L** signposted *Winsford*. Go through a gate onto a broad stone track and shortly fork **R** onto the upper track by a severely pruned oak tree. Shortly after the summit, at a X-roads of tracks turn **L** onto tarmac signposted *Winsford*.

3 **Easy to miss:** after 800m keep an eye out for a blue paint waymark on a bridlegate off to the **L**, set back from the road, adjacent to a metal field gate (GR 908316). Go through the gate onto a climbing grassy track with ever better views. Go through a bridlegate after passing *Highercombe Farm* buildings to your left and follow signs for *Tarr Steps* diagonally **R** on a grassy track.

4 Follow the track to the road, turn **R**, cross the cattlegrid then opposite the second road on the left (to *Tarr Steps*) turn **R** downhill onto a grassy track, with a line of trees to your **R**. There is the occasional blue paint waymark on trees.

5 Follow to the wall corner and continue downhill towards woodland on a better red gravel track. Follow with a line of trees to the left. At a metal gate go into the field to the **L** via a bridlegate, leaving the main stone track. Follow the **left-hand** field edge around two sides of the field, **ignoring** two bridlegates in the corner of the field. Take the **next** gate on the **L**, opposite a *Week Lane / Tarr Steps* signpost.

6 Descend on a steep, at times narrow track signposted *Bridleway* through a pheasant-rearing area and down through woodland, deciduous then conifer. You are aiming towards *Yellowcombe Cottage*, tucked away in the woods. Ford the stream near the footbridge and turn **R** through a gate to join a wider track. Climb then descend on a bedrock rollercoaster track.

7 At the T-junction with the road turn **R** down into *Winsford*. At the T-junction just past the *Royal Oak* PH turn **R** then shortly **R** again in the centre of the village signposted *Dulverton, Minehead*.

8 On a left-hand bend at the start of a sharp climb turn **R** onto a track by a house signposted *RUPP to Edbrook, Hill Gate*. Very steep climb. At the fork bear **R** signposted *Week Lane*. At the T-junction with the road turn **R**. Climb. **Easy to miss:** shortly after the summit turn **L** through a gravel parking area and a metal gate onto a wide grassy track (GR 906329).

9 At the end of the field turn **R** through a gate signposted *Bridleway*. Amazingly overgrown enclosed track OR use the field edge to the **R** of this, dropping down to a broad stone track with a stream in the valley below. Turn **L** then fork **R** by the ruin onto the lower track. Cross the stream near to the pumping engine. Climb then leave the main track and turn **R** uphill through a gate into field by a *Bridleway* signpost.

10 Follow the **right-hand** field edge to the top, turn **R** through the gate then **L** onto a broad stone track. At the junction of several tracks by a farm turn **R** onto a level track to go past a large tree. Go round a sharp left-hand bend, climb, then at a T-junction with a similar broad track turn **R** to continue uphill.

11 At the X-roads turn **L** signposted *Dulverton* to rejoin the outward route. Continue on the main track, **ignoring** the track to the right you climbed up from *Dulverton*. Great descent, some muddy patches. Emerge at *School Lane* by *Rock House Inn*, and turn **R** to return to the start.

PHOTO: ANDY HEADING

PHOTO: NICK COTTON

EXMOOR CAN BE TWEE... PHOTO: NICK COTTON

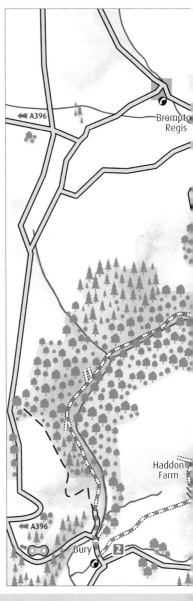

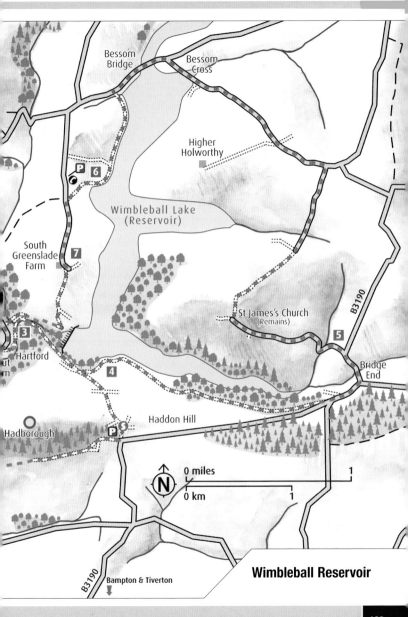

Wimbleball Reservoir

PHOTO: ANDY HEADING

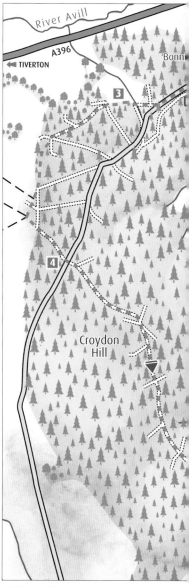

Carhampton

DUNSTER

B3191

A39

BRIDGWATER
& M5 ➡

2

6

5

0 miles 1

Ⓝ

0 km 1

Carhampton &
Croydon Hill

MONKSILVER & BROMPTON RALPH

GRADE:

DISTANCE: 19KM   **TOTAL ASCENT:** 400M

START/FINISH: MONKSILVER   **GRID REFERENCE:** 075375

PARKING: MONKSILVER COMMUNITY HALL CAR PARK, ON THE STOGUMBER ROAD ON THE SOUTHEAST EDGE OF THE VILLAGE GR 075375

CAFÉ: RALEGH'S CROSS HOTEL, 1.3KM WEST OF ROUTE ALONG THE B3224 Tel: 01984 640 343

PUBLIC HOUSE: NOTLEY ARMS, MONKSILVER Tel: 01984 656 217

ROCK 'N' ROLL! **PHOTO:** ANDY HEADING

Monksilver
& Brompton Ralph – Exmoor

Introduction

Tucked into the eastern corner of the National Park, this ride just gets better and better as it goes on – and the final descent down into **Monksilver** will have you gagging to come back and do it again.

The Ride

A steep road climb at the start with fine views east to the **Quantocks** brings you to **Ashbeer** and the first off-road descent, steep and fast at its end. Meander your way down Somerset lanes to the hamlet of **Brompton Ralph** and the start of the next track - one of those smooth bedrock trails that must have seen the wheels of a thousand farm waggons in times past. Climb to the mast, follow tracks past **Sedgeborough** and *Fryan Farms* through to the busy(ish) *B3224* where you may wish to turn left for 5 minutes to refuel at *Ralegh's Cross Hotel*. If not, prepare for the best bit of the ride, first the amazing views west to the folds and combes and patchwork of fields of the National Park and then on for the wonderful woodland descent, dropping 200m down to **Monksilver**.

Making a day of it

No rides are nearby - jump back in the car and head west to **Carhampton** or east to the **Quantocks**, just as close by.

Sedgeborough Farm

Fryan Farm

6

5

4

3

Brompton Ralph

WIVELISCOMBE

**Monksilver &
Brompton Ralph**

Directions — Monksilver & Brompton Ralph

1 From the *Community Hall* car park turn **L** uphill. Follow signs for *Stogumber*, ignoring turns to right and left. Just beyond the brow of the hill and the mast, bear **R** at a road junction by a triangle of grass then shortly turn **R** onto a track immediately after a house on the right signposted *RUPP to Elworthy*.

2 Good track, at times a bit overgrown, ending with good stone descent on a sunken track. At the road turn **L**. At the X-roads with the *B3224* go **SA**, descend, then after a brief climb take the first road to the **R** by a gnarly old oak tree (no sign). **Ignore** a road to the right then, at the T-junction, turn **R** downhill.

3 Go past the church, go down into *Brompton Ralph* then opposite the telephone box and just before the village stores turn **R** and shortly **R** again onto a track climbing to the **R** of a house with a 'potter' shadow on the wall. Bedrock track.

4 Up and down. At the T-junction with the road bear **L** uphill alongside a line of telegraph poles. Climb steeply on tarmac passing a small plantation of trees to the **L**. At the T-junction at the top by a triangle of grass with a mast to your right turn **L** onto a broad gravel track.

5 At the offset X-roads with tarmac turn **L** then **R**. The track turns sharp **R**, becomes grass and drops down to go past *Sedgeborough Farm*. Go through a dip and up **L** into the field aiming for the top **L** corner of the field and going through the newer metal gate leading onto a track towards the barn.

6 Pass to the **L** of *Fryan Farm* buildings going through a gate and onto the tarmac drive. At the road turn **L**. At the T-junction with the *B3224* turn **L** signposted *Ralegh's Cross* then take the first road to the **R** signposted *Colton Lane*.

7 After 1km, on a sharp right-hand bend go **SA** through a bridlegate onto a track sign-posted *Bridleway to Chidgeley*. Stay on the right-hand edge of the field as vast views open up to the left down to the hamlets of *Leighland Chapel* and *Stamborough*. Go through the gate following blue waymarks then through a second gate leading into the woodland and onto a good stone track. As this track turns downhill on a sharp left-hand hairpin bend, bear **R** slightly uphill signposted *Monksilver via Colton*.

8 At a T-junction with a broader track at the top of the climb go **SA** through the gate ahead into and across the field (blue waymarks) to a gate onto the road. Turn **L**. At a T-junction by a triangle of grass go **SA** into woodland through a wooden field gate signposted *Wildlife Conservation Area*.

9 Great descent! At the T-junction with the road by *Lime Walk Cottage* turn **R**. At the T-junction with the main road through the village turn **R** then shortly, on a sharp right-hand bend bear **L** signposted *Stogumber* to return to the start.

PHOTO: ANDY HEADING

SECTION 3

Quantocks

The Quantock Hills are like Doctor Who's Tardis. From the map they look like a tiny range, about 16km long by 8km wide, that could barely provide a morning's ride let alone a full day out - but once you are there you could keep exploring for weeks. There are literally hundreds of kilometres of tracks including a big slab of Forestry Commission woodland on the east side of the ridge that offers trails for every type of riding.

Quantocks
sponsored by SHIMANO

www.ultimatepursuits.co.uk

It must be said that the **Quantocks**, more so than most other areas, demand intimate local knowledge that can only come from riding and re-riding each and every one of the tracks, up and down, winter and summer, wet and dry and – if you are equipped for it – day and night. There are many more tracks on the ground than you will find on even the most detailed map and this, combined with the distinct scarcity of signs, means that route finding is based as much on accumulated experience as on map reading and following route instructions.

Two things are almost guaranteed when you go mountain biking in the **Quantocks** for the first time: first, you will have an eye-opening, big buzz of a ride and second, you will get lost. Even the ridge ride, which ought to be easy-peasy in terms of finding your way, has a couple of places where you may well suddenly find yourself shooting a long way off on the wrong tangent. Losing your way is hardly ever a big deal as the tracks are so plentiful that it is never too hard to find an alternative route back up to or down from the ridge – and almost all of them stay in good condition. The one **no-no** is to use the **A39** to link up different ends of a ride: it is a very busy, unpleasant, narrow twisty A road with poor visibility and high hedgerows. Not much chance of survival for a flock of mountain bikers should two milk lorries happen to meet on a blind bend!

The rides described in the **Quantocks** give you a framework around which you can elaborate and embroider. The obvious feature of the area is the 11km ridge track, wide and stone-based with fantastic views almost along its entire length. Most of the rides are joined to this like ribs to a spinal column. The climbs on the north side tend to be easier and more plentiful than those on the south side. Go with plenty of time and an open mind to explore and you could be there for weeks!

BIG SKY, QUANTOCKS RIDGE **PHOTO:** ANDY HEADING

The Quantocks Ridge (linear) — Quantocks

Introduction

A real 'roof of the world' ride, undulating between 300m and 350m. Do this easy introduction to the **Quantocks** on a fine day as the views are stupendous. It is the backbone of the **Quantocks** and almost all other rides hang off it, or use part of it. Good, year-round riding and a great ride to introduce novices to the joys of mountain biking.

The ride

You might expect it to be impossible to get lost on a ridge ride: think again! The **Quantocks** are criss-crossed with loads of tracks not shown on the map and there are very few signposts or waymarks, so it really is worth taking a good look around you at each junction of tracks to get your bearings for the return. The eastern half of the ride is among high banks of beech trees, the western half is more open among the gorse and heather of the heathland. The trig point on *Beacon Hill* above **Quantoxhead** is a natural turnaround point with excellent 360 degree views.

Making a day of it

The *Holford* and *Aisholt* rides overlap with the ridge ride; the ride starting at **Enmore** comes to within 1km of the *Lydeard Hill* car park, at *Cothelstone Hill*.

THE QUANTOCKS RIDGE (LINEAR)	GRADE: ▲

DISTANCE: 11KM EACH WAY (ie 22km round trip)   **TOTAL ASCENT:** 130M EACH WAY (ie 260m total)

START/FINISH: LYDEARD HILL CAR PARK, NORTH OF BISHOPS LYDEARD

GRID REFERENCE: 181337   **PARKING:** AS OPPOSITE (GR 181337)

CAFÉ: BRING SANDWICHES

PUBLIC HOUSE: NONE ON THE RIDGE. RISING SUN, WEST BAGBOROUGH IS NEAREST Tel: 01823 432 575

Directions – The Quantocks Ridge (Linear)

1   Exit the car park via a gate onto a wide stone track heading northwest. After 1.5km, at a fork by a *Footpath no bikes* signpost pointing left, bear **R** and keep bearing **R** around the rim of the valley/combe to your right until reaching the woodland by a stone wall. Turn **L** here (GR 171354) and have a good look around for recognisable features for your return trip, this is one of two places where it is very easy to take the wrong track on the way back - and end up a long way down the hill!

2   Go through a car park with a cattle grid and a road to your right. After a further 2.5km go **SA** at a X-roads with a lane (GR 150375). Follow the obvious sunken track northwest. After 300m, at a major junction of tracks by the white gateway of *Crowcombe Park Gate* to your left, bear **L** on the lower track.

3   Climb then descend to a tall wooden post with metal spike (*Halsway Soggs*). Have a good look around you to remember this point for the return. Continue **SA** in the same direction (northwest) on the broad stone track, generally following *Motor Vehicles* wooden signposts.

4   Maintain height and continue in the same direction on the most obvious broad, stone-based track for a further 3km. At the one major fork of level, stone-based tracks where there is a possibility of taking the wrong turn, bear **R** (GR 128405). You will soon see the trig point (up to the left). Climb up to this for fabulous all round views and retrace your steps.

The Quantocks Ridge
(Linear)

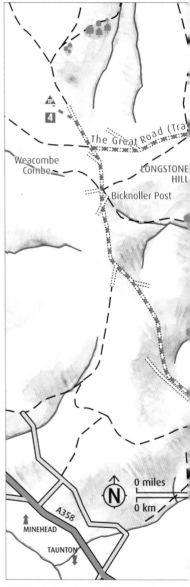

The Great Road (Tra

Weacombe
Combe

LONGSTONE
HILL

Bicknoller Post

4

0 miles

0 km

N

A358

MINEHEAD

TAUNTON

PHOTO: ANDY HEADING

MINEHEAD

Holford

P S

A39

BRIDGWATER

Hotel

Holford Combe

2

Halsway
Post

Halsway
Doggs

Black Hill

1
1

CROWCOMBE

Dead Woman's
Ditch

**Holford &
the Great Road**

Directions – Holford & the Great Road

1 Exit *Holford* car park, turn **R** then take the first road to the **R** sharply back on your-self signposted *Holford Combe*. After 800m the tarmac turns to track by the hotel. Keep following the track close to the stream, crossing and recrossing as necessary.

2 After 1.6km the main track narrows and divides. Take the more defined **left-hand** track. Steep 10-minute climb. At a T-junction of tracks at the top turn **R** then at the T-junction with the road turn **R** again. At the *Dead Woman's Ditch* road sign turn **R** signposted *Crowcombe* then shortly take the 1st broad track to the **R**.

For a short cut back to Holford.
After almost 1.5km, shortly after a fast down then up, at a major X-roads of tracks (GR 148384) turn **R** along the track leading along a ridge towards *Black Hill*. Good stone and grass descent. After the first houses on the left follow the track round to the **L** to emerge in *Holford* car park.

3 At the major junction of six tracks at *Halsway Soggs* by a tall round post with a metal spike through it and a low square post with *Motor vehicles* on it bear **R** on the furthest right of the tracks. Basically follow red arrows and *Motor Vehicles* signposts for 3km. Route finding is a bit tricky between *Bicknoller Post* (GR 128404) and the crossing of the *Great Road*: **ignore** a track signposted *No vehicles* to the right then shortly at the next fork, with steep-sided *Weacombe Combe* down to your left, take the **right-hand** track. Continue to the trig point (up on your left).

4 On the descent from the trig point, return along the ridge, bearing **L** to join the *Great Road* (a wide stone track) which descends ENE towards woodland. Aim to join the corner of the woodland (GR 145411) by a holly tree, a beech tree, a gorse bush and a *No vehicles* signpost! Follow this main track down through woodland to the road and turn **R** to return to the car park.

AISHOLT & THE SOUTHERN COMBES   GRADE:

DISTANCE: 16KM   **TOTAL ASCENT:** 480M

START/FINISH: HAWKRIDGE RESERVOIR CAR PARK, SW OF SPAXTON

GRID REFERENCE: 206361   **PARKING:** AS OPPOSITE (GR 206361)

CAFÉ: BRING SANDWICHES

PUBLIC HOUSE: RISING SUN INN, WEST BAGBOROUGH Tel: 01823 432 575

PHOTO: *ANDY HEADING*

Aisholt & the Southern Combes – Quantocks

Introduction

Long easy climb, testing descent, great pub, impossible climb (now there is a challenge!), a taste of the famous **Quantocks** ridge and a second long open descent gives you the idea. As ever on the **Quantocks**, the options to extend a ride like this are infinite.

The ride

The road around the reservoir at the start is flat - it makes a nice contrast to the rest of the ride. An easy woodland track (which can get muddy) drops you at the bottom of a steep road climb through the hamlet of **Aisholt**. Once off-road the gradient eases briefly before steepening again - did you say let's stop to look at the view? The ridge is reached and a sneaky parallel bridleway keeps you away from the traffic heading for the car park. Barely have you time to savour the ridge before the steepest descent of the day beckons. Shake, rattle and roll your way down to the fine pub in **West Bagborough**, take it easy on the lanes then head back up onto the ridge. You pushed your bike? You won't be the first! ...or the last. Back on top you may wish to extend the ride by linking along the ridge to the *Holford and the Great Road* ride. Otherwise it's a long swoop around the rim of the steep-sided combe to your right - then a slightly less manic descent on loose rock, or parallel grass, or woodland tracks back to the reservoir.

Making a day of it

The ridge ride links this circuit to the Ride 2: *Holford and the Great Road* at the northwest end of the ridge. Alternatively, upon reaching the road at the top of the long climb up from the reservoir via **Luxborough** you could turn left and link to Ride 4: *Enmore and Cothelstone Hill*.

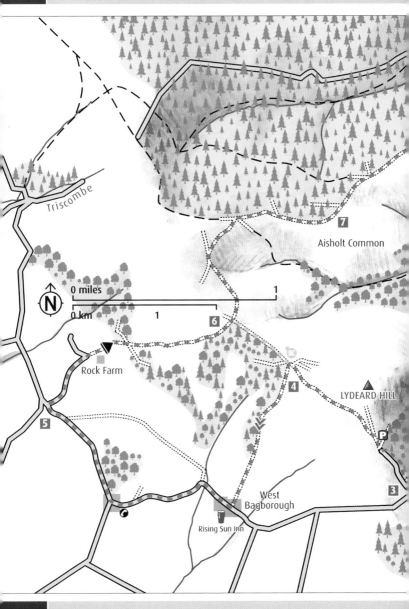

Triscombe

Aisholt Common

7

N
0 miles _____ 1
0 km _____ 1

6

Rock Farm

4

LYDEARD HILL

P

5

3

West
Bagborough

Rising Sun Inn

Aisholt & the Southern Combes

Directions – Aisholt & the Southern Combes

1 From the car park by *Hawkridge Reservoir* follow the road westwards with the water to your right. At the T-junction turn **R** signposted *Over Stowey, Nether Stowey*. Cross the dam wall then turn **L** downhill by a house called *Martindale*. Follow two *Bridleway* signposts onto a climbing track ahead.

2 At the road turn **L** steeply uphill, passing *Aisholt Church*. Soon after the gradient eases turn first **R** uphill onto a no through road. The tarmac turns to track. Continue climbing to the top with huge views opening up to the left.

3 At the T-junction with the road turn **R** onto a parallel wooded track signposted *Bridleway*. Go through the car park onto the obvious wide stone track beyond the gate with fantastic views to the south and west. After 800m go through a gate and turn **L*** steeply downhill by a red arrow signposted *Vehicles*.

    * ⟩OR⟩ for a short cut continue **SA**.

4 Fast, loose rock descent with several round grey concrete pipes across the path. The track drops you down and right by the *Rising Sun Inn, West Bagborough*. Turn **R** on the road for 1km then turn first **R** after the telephone box onto a road called *Heathfield*, signposted *Triscombe*.

5 After a further 1km take the first road to the **R** signposted with an *exclamation mark!* The tarmac turns to track. Go through a gate and fork **R** onto a steep and stony track. After crossing a forestry track the surface becomes easier and the gradient slightly less steep.

6 Emerge from the woodland onto a wide open grassy heather area with gravel tracks. Do **not** go left uphill on an obvious track but continue **SA** contouring around the hillside. At a fork of tracks bear **R** towards the forest* then follow this track alongside the woodland, with the trees to your left

* ➤OR to extend the ride, turn **L** once you reach the wall at the edge of the forest and follow the ridge northwest to the trigpoint on *Beacon Hill*, above *Quantoxhead*.

7 There are more options for this descent than are shown on the map! The main track is a loose stone descent but there are other parallel tracks to the right or just inside the woodland. Take your pick. The track turns to tarmac. Continue downhill in the same direction. At the T-junction by a road signpost turn **R** towards *Taunton, Bridgwater* (GR 199363). Rejoin the outward route and turn **L** after crossing the dam wall to return to the car park at the start.

PHOTO: ANDY HEADING

GIB HILL

Lambridge
Farm

4

5

COTHELSTONE
HILL

Buncombe Wood

3

6

Cothelstone

Ivyton Farm

8

7

KINGSTON ST. MARY

**Enmore &
Cothelstone Hill**

Directions – Enmore & Cothelstone Hill

1 With your back to the *Tynte Arms* PH in *Enmore*, turn **L** uphill. Climb for 1.5km on this busyish road. Go past a house called *Hillandale* on the left. Shortly after a 'Right turn ahead' road sign turn **R**, signposted *No through road for motor vehicles*. Go downhill and follow the tarmac round to the **L**. Shortly fork **R** off the tarmac onto a track by the gate (red arrow waymark).

2 Descend then climb. This track will be muddy in winter or after prolonged rain. Join tarmac and continue climbing. At the T-junction with the road (there is a round mirror ahead) turn **L** then take the 2nd road to the **R** opposite the tall round metal grain silo and barns.

3 At a T-junction with a letter box in the wall to the right bear **L** then, shortly after going round a sharp left-hand bend and passing a pink house on the right, turn **R** onto a no through road.

4 Go through the farm. The gradient steepens dramatically. **Ignore** a right turn and bear **L** as the tarmac turns to track and continues uphill through two gates. Keep the hedge to your left.

5 Fabulous, very English views. Exit the field into woodland in the top left-hand corner. Follow the track for 100m to a X-roads of tracks, turn **R** uphill then **easy to miss:** after 200m, on a wide left-hand bend, turn R onto a narrow track. Emerge at tarmac by a junction of roads and turn **L*** then **R** onto a path that goes directly away from road signposted The Rap.

* ▶ For a link to the *Quantocks* ridge and the *Aisholt* and *Holford* rides, turn **R** and climb steeply to the popular *Lydeard Hill* car park (GR 181338), gateway to the *Quantocks* ridge.

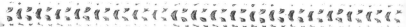

6   Superb quality surface, occasionally overgrown. After 1km, **Ignore** the first major track to the right, sharply downhill (with a blue arrow on a wooden post). Shortly **ignore** a second right on a footpath (*Macmillan Way*). Continue in the same direction bearing **R** along the edge of the woodland. This becomes a fast descent. **Easy to miss:** at the first obvious clearing by a signpost (GR 199307) turn sharp **L** (blue arrow). Follow the track round a sharp left-hand bend.

7   Climb then go round a right-hand bend. Go through a farm onto tarmac. After a short climb, on a sharp left-hand bend, turn **R** downhill on a broad stone track signposted *Quantocks Greenway*.

8   Testing sunken descent through woodland. At the road go **SA** onto the track opposite to continue downhill. Cross a ford and climb on a very narrow overgrown and steep track. Another big track joins from the right. At the T-junction with the road by the telephone box turn **R** then shortly **L** by a *Broomfield, Fyne Court* signpost.

9   About 800m after passing *Broomfield Church*, on a sharp left-hand bend on a down-hill section just after the *Old Vicarage* (to your left) bear **R** onto a track and take the left-hand of three tracks, signposted *Quantocks Greenway*. Great track.

10   At the road turn **L**. **Ignore** a right turn on a sharp, left-hand bend. At the top of the long climb turn **L** then **R** (signposted *Quantocks Greenway*) through a field gate onto a track. Superb open descent on a field edge track with views out to sea. Reddish earth path. After 1.5km, at a red brick, red-tiled old barn with the road in sight ahead, turn sharp **L** onto a track. At the road turn **R**. At the T-junction with the more major road by *Enmore Primary School* turn **R** to return to the start.

The Mendips

*The Mendips are a whaleback-shaped ridge
of carboniferous limestone stretching east
from Weston-super-Mare to beyond Shepton
Mallet, with the Cheddar Gorge as its most
famous landmark. The best mountain biking
trails lie to the north of Cheddar up over
Black Down (the highest point on the
Mendips) towards Burrington Combe.
Two other rides should be mentioned -
the first follows the ridge running west
from the A38 at King's Wood over Wavering
Down towards Crook Peak and over the M5
to Bleadon Hill; the second explores the
bridleways and byways to the northeast
and northwest of Wells.*

The Mendips
sponsored by

www.ultimatepursuits.co.uk

BONUS RIDE

The Mendips offer outstanding riding – some of the best in the South West. They are a very conveniently located range of hills, close to the M5 and less than 20km from **Bristol**. There is a great variety of terrain – the forestry area of **Rowberrow Warren** alone has around 25km of rocky woodland trail – whilst the jewel in the crown, **Black Down**, has steep hillsides that are laced with the sweetest of singletrack. You will enjoy this at it's best during the summer as you snake across the hillside through shoulder high bracken.

The exposed **Mendips plateau** can feel surprisingly high and remote considering the fact that the starting points are located in such gentile countryside, but in actual fact you are seldom more than a half dozen or so kilometres from a good source of tea and cakes! A good alternative start for rides in these hills is the main car park at the bottom of **Burrington Combe**, next to **Burrington Inn** (GR ST476587). The descent back to the car park across the shoulder of **Beacon Batch** and then down **Burrington Ham** gets a double thumbs-up for quality!

Look out for the excellent **Black Down and Rowberrow Forest MTB trail guide** – a superb, laminated map with colour coded (graded) bridleways, available from the **Mendip Hills Area of Outstanding Natural Beauty Service**, telephone 01761 462 338.

Directions – Cheddar Challenge
Bonus Ride

Start: the *Edelweiss Restaurant*, opposite the *Cheddar Caves Information Booth* at the lower end of Cheddar's main street.

1 From the *Edelweiss Restaurant*, take the narrow lane rising out of *Cheddar* (to the left of St Andrews Road).

2 At T-junction turn **L** for 300m to *Bradley Cross*, indicated by a sign and red letter box. Turn **L** then **R**, following a blue-signed bridleway towards *Draycott*.

3 Follow this grassy track into open fields, with occasional blue arrows and with fine views out over the *Somerset Levels* behind. Continue uphill through gate with two large wooden posts. Climb steeply on narrow stony track, joining a farm track and then, at a T-junction, a better, level track. Follow this pleasantly, eventually descending to the road.

4 A fast, tarmac section now begins. At X-roads with road (B3135) continue **SA** signposted *Compton Martin, Harptree*. After 1.6km take first road **L**, signposted *Charterhouse*. At X-roads near to *Charterhouse* church continue **SA**, then after 800m take first **L** on bridleway towards mast.

5 Keep to **left** of the mast. At trig point continue in same direction, heading towards the top of the distant plantation. Great singletrack, but can be a little soft in places during the winter through to late spring. Some 500m past the trig point, take a distinct **R** fork. The singletrack descends gently to the gate at the boundary of the plantation.

6 Go through the gate, **SA** for 50m, then **R** taking the broad, rocky, straight descent through woodland. **Ignore** minor tracks off to the left and, at the next major junction, go **SA**. Take the **L** track at the next major junction.

7 **Easy to miss:** after 1.6km, in a small clearing with a green gate ahead and on your left, turn **L** passing a field then stables on the right.

8 Pass the pink, white and cream houses on your left, keeping to unmetalled track. At X-roads of bridleways continue **SA** following blue arrow signs for *Cheddar*.

9 Cross stream to your left and join forestry track coming up from left. At X-roads of tracks continue **SA** to *Tynings Farm*. Through farm to road.

10 At road continue **SA**, with wall on right. After 300m, as road bends **R**, continue **SA** signposted *Road Unsuitable for Motor Vehicles*.

11 Where this bears left into quarry, continue **SA** down steep, challenging bridlepath into *Cheddar*. In the open field, take the broad track to the **L** and follow the main track as it bends round to T-junction with road.

12 Turn **R** on road (Hannay Road) then first **L** (Kent Street) to return to start.

PHOTO: ANDY HEADING

Appendixes

Tourist Information Centres

Dartmoor
Okehampton	Tel: 01837 53020
Tavistock	Tel: 01822 612938
Newton Abbot	Tel: 01626 367494

Exmoor
Lynton	Tel: 01598 752225
Minehead	Tel: 01643 702624
South Molton	Tel: 01769 574122
Porlock Visitor Centre	Tel: 01643 863150

Quantocks
Bridgwater	Tel: 01278 427652
Taunton	Tel: 01823 336344

Weather
www.bbc.co.uk/weather   www.metoffice.com

Accommodation -
Youth Hostels
Dartmoor
Okehampton	Tel: 0870 770 5692
Bellever	Tel: 0870 770 5978
Steps Bridge	Tel: 0870 770 6048

Exmoor
Lynton	Tel: 0870 770 5942
Minehead	Tel: 0870 770 5972
Exford	Tel: 0870 770 5828

Quantocks
Crowcombe	Tel: 0870 770 5782
Quantock Hills	Tel: 01278 741224
	OR 01629 592708

Other accommodation
I had a rough run of luck during my research and with the exception of Exmoor House in Porlock could not really recommend any of the places I stayed at.

There is a good brochure called **'Stay on a Farm' www.farmstayuk.co.uk** which is reasonably sound.

Lynmouth / Lynton produce an accommodation guide covering most of Exmoor. Phone the TIC (01598 752225) or visit **www.lyntourism.co.uk**

Food and Drink
The pubs I visited were in the evening when I was clean. I could not say how pubs might react to a bunch of muddy bikers (except in the garden, of course). I don't know that I would add any more than is contained in the barebones information for each ride. Surely the punters are interested primarily in the ride and a good pub is a bonus. Your views?

Bike Shops -
Exmoor & the Quantocks

With the exception of Pompys in Minehead there is no bike shop close to the rides themselves. The nearest bike stores are in Barnstaple, Tiverton, Bridgwater and Taunton.

Minehead
Pompys Cycle Shop, Mart Road, Minehead.
Tel: **01643 704077**

Barnstaple
Cyril Webster, 50-51 Bear Street, Barnstaple.
Tel: **01271 343277**
Bike Shed, The Square, Barnstaple.
Tel: **01271 328628**
Bike It Ltd, 65 Newport Road, Barnstaple.
Tel 01271 323873
Planet Bike Ltd, Unit 47 Upcott Avenue,
Barnstaple. Tel: **01271 327455**

Tiverton
Maynards Cycle Shop, 25 Gold Street, Tiverton.
Tel: **01884 253979**
Rons Cycle Centre, 10 Wellbrook Street, Tiverton.
Tel: **01884 255750**

Bridgwater
Somerset Cycles, Rodway, Cannington,
Bridgwater. Tel: **01278 655191**
The Bicycle Chain, Herswell Business Pk, Salmon
Pde, Bridgwater. Tel: **01278 423640**
St. John Street Cycles, 91-93 St. John St,
Bridgwater. Tel: **01278 441516**

Bargain Bikes, 36 St. John Street, Bridgwater.
Tel: **01278 444418**
Scorpion CS, 3 Nythe Rd, Pedwell, Bridgwater.
Tel: **01458 211166**

Taunton
Ralph Colman Cycles, 79 Station Rd, Taunton.
Tel: **01823 275822**
Kings Cycles, 38 Station Rd, Taunton.
Tel: **01823 352272**
Ians Cycle Centre, 3 Roman Road, Taunton.
Tel: **01823 283631**
The Bicycle Chain, Chip La, Staple Grove Rd,
Taunton. Tel: **01823 252499**
The Playground, 25 Bridge St, Taunton.
Tel: **01823 251511**

Bike Shops - Dartmoor
Okehampton
Moor Cycles, The Arcade, Fore St, Okehampton.
Tel: **01837 659677**

Newton Abbot
Bigpeaks Com Ltd, Eastern Rd, Linhay Business
Pk, Newton Abbot. Tel: **01364 654103**

South Brent
TC2 Recycles, 9 Station Rd, South Brent.
Tel: **01364 73221**

Tavistock
Tavistock Cycles, Farriers Ct, Paddons Rw,
Tavistock. Tel: **01822 617630**

Plymouth

Halfords Ltd, Unit 4, Marsh Mills Pk, Plymouth.
Tel: 01752 224006
Recycles Mobile Cycle Services, 17 Eastbury Av,
Plymouth. Tel: 01752 513991
A1 Bicycles, The Workshop, 28 Biggin Hl,
Plymouth. Tel: 01752 369369
Bike, 2 Pemros Rd, Plymouth.
Tel: 01752 366988
Devon Cycles, 2 Frankfort Gte, Plymouth.
Tel: 01752 664771
Plymouth Cycle Scene, Hyde Pk Ho, Mutley
Plain, Plymouth. Tel: 01752 257701
Halfords Ltd, 15 Cornwall St, Plymouth.
Tel: 01752 661652
Battery Cycle Works. 52-56 Embankment Rd,
Plymouth. Tel: 01752 665553
Natural Cycles. 100 Albert Rd, Plymouth.
Tel: 01752 550729
The Bike Cellar, 13a Radford Park Rd, Plymouth.
Tel: 01752 408338

Bike Hire -
Exmoor & the Quantocks
Barnstaple

Bike Trail Cycle Hire, Fremington Stn,
Fremington, Barnstaple. Tel: 01271 372586
Tarka Trail Cycle Hire, Barnstaple Railway Stn,
Station Rd, Sticklepath, Barnstaple.
Tel: 01271 324202

Taunton

Kings Cycles, 38 Station Rd, Taunton.
Tel: 01823 352272

Outdoor Shops -
Exmoor & the Quantocks
Barnstaple

Cassies Army & Navy, Rolles Qy, Barnstaple.
Tel: 01271 345079
No Sweat Outdoors, 103 High St, Barnstaple.
Tel: 01271 372668
Millets, 91 High St, Barnstaple.
Tel: 01271 342937

Taunton

The Wearhouse Ltd, 32 North St, Taunton.
Tel: 01823 333291

Millets, 20 East St, Taunton.
Tel: 01823 332782

Bridgwater

Millets, 5 Fore St, Bridgwater.
Tel: 01278 422243

Bike Hire - Dartmoor
Okehampton

OK Leisure, 34 Fore St, Okehampton.
Tel: 01837 52725

Exeter

Taunton Leisure Ltd, 110 Fore St, Exeter.
Tel: 01392 410534
Millets, 207 High St, Exeter.
Tel: 01392 255811
Moorland Rambler, 148-149 Fore St, Exeter.
Tel: 01392 432681
Blacks Camping & Leisure Ltd, 181 Sidwell St,
Exeter. Tel: 01392 276423

Newton Abbot

Millets, 2 Queen St, Newton Abbot.
Tel: **01626 353405**

Ashburton

Trail Venture, 7 North St, Ashburton, Newton
Abbot. Tel: **01364 652522**

Plymouth

Millets, 40 New George St, Plymouth.
Tel: **01752 665521**

Tavistock

Kountry Kit Ltd, 22-23 West St, Tavistock.
Tel: **01822 613089**

Other publications

Dartmoor for off-road cyclists map (£9.95).
Dartmoor National Park. Fine waterproof mountain biking map highlighting bridleways all over
Dartmoor with different colours to indicate the
difficulty of the tracks. Available from local bike
shops, Tourist Information Centres or from the
National Park itself: **Dartmoor National Park
Authority**, High Moorland Visitor Centre, Old
Duchy Hotel, Princetown, Yelverton, Devon PL20
6QF. Tel: **01822 890414**. There is an online shop
on their website: **www.dartmoor-npa.gov.uk**
You will have to pay £9.95 + £2.95 p&tp for the
map if you want it mailed to you.

**Exmoor, North Devon & the Quantocks
(Goldeneye)** (£5.99) Laminated map with 10
routes described, two lie west of Exmoor on the
coast near Woolacombe, six are on Exmoor and
two are on the Quantocks. Available on-line at:
www.goldeneyemaps.com

About the author

Nick Cotton has written over 30 bike guides in
the last 12 years, riding more than 20,000 miles
all over Britain during the course of his research.
He has travelled and trekked extensively, climbing
to over 18,000ft in three continents and has
cycled in Morocco and Patagonia (the worst
winds in the world!) In an earlier life he imported
wooden snakes from South America. He has
recently moved with his family from Bristol to
Cumbria to be closer to the hills.

About the photographer –
Andy Heading

A professional sports photographer, Andy's 20
years as a mountain biker have included trips to
Ethiopia, Romania, Morocco and China, and rac-
ing wins in Polaris, Trailquest and the 1,097-mile
Iditasport Impossible across Alaska.

Vertebrate Graphics

Vertebrate Graphics is Britain's leading graphic
design agency that specialises in the outdoor
leisure market. We have had substantial success
in the design and production of specialist
outdoor books. These include **Hillwalking –
The Official Handbook of the Mountain
Leader and Walking Group Leader schemes**
(a best-selling outdoor title for two years running),
and two highly praised guidebooks for rock
climbers - **Selected Rock Climbs in The Lake
District** and **Staffordshire Gritstone**.